Under the Laurel Tree

Grieving Infertility
with Saints Joachim and Anna

NICOLE M. ROCCAS

ANCIENT FAITH PUBLISHING

CHESTERTON, INDIANA

Published by:
  Ancient Faith Publishing
  A Division of Ancient Faith Ministries
  P.O. Box 748
  Chesterton, IN 46304

Icon on cover and page 4 by Mother Olga of Romania.

ISBN: 978-1-944967-69-7

Printed in the United States of America

Library of Congress Control Number:2019950189

DISCLAIMER

Infertility is a highly sensitive, personal, and at times controversial subject. While everything in this book is true, the narrative elements may not be factual in the literal sense. In the case of anecdotes from my own life, I have occasionally compressed characters and events or otherwise altered their retelling to uphold readability and the privacy of others. To preserve the anonymity of respondents to the Under the Laurel Tree Questionnaire, I have removed all identifying information and attributed quotations to pseudonyms with the consent of participants.

In writing about the spiritual struggle of infertility and the lives of Saints Joachim and Anna, I do not purport to speak as a theologian or academic authority, but as an honest pilgrim trying to learn what it means to lead a life of meaning in the midst of loss.

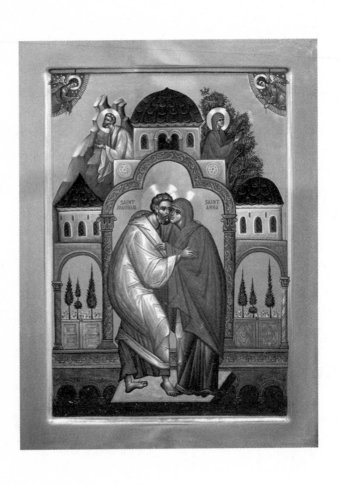

To our nephew, Tobias Lee,
himself a long-awaited miracle,
and our dear godson, Yianni,
both of whom were born while this book was being written
and have reminded us anew of God's unending faithfulness:

May God grant you and those who love you
many precious years.

Contents

Foreword

*W*here *most of us live,* there are no snowflakes in September. Yet it is with this kind of "inconceivable" occurrence that Dr. Nicole Roccas, whom I consider a dear colleague, begins her remarkable book, *Under the Laurel Tree.* Hurrying to a Divine Liturgy one September morning, she spotted a lone snowflake "falling from heaven to earth." While others bustled mindlessly past, she saw in that glimmer a much-needed reminder that "seasons change; that no matter how long the sun-scorched droughts of faith or famine may last, they will not last forever; that somehow behind and amid all things is a God who is mysteriously, perplexingly good."

We don't expect snowflakes in September, and married couples don't expect infertility when they want to have children. Nicole is all too aware of the shock and anguish that set in when conception proves difficult; she and her husband have been dealing with infertility for over five years. This is a grief that, as she acknowledges, takes "your expectations for how the world works—and life, and marriage—and turns them inside out. And in the grief, the struggle will come to be about much more than what is or isn't growing in one's womb."

Avoiding superficial answers, *Under the Laurel Tree* gets to the heart of the mental, spiritual, and interpersonal issues at stake in infertility, including difficult topics like marital strain and the inappropriate comments of others. All the while, however, we are led to the truth that God challenges our expectations and provides peace and joy as only He can, in His way. By combining pearls of wisdom from the Bible and other revered sources with astute observations and interviews, Nicole integrates the experience of infertility with faith in a life-giving God.

Woven throughout *Under the Laurel Tree* is the intimate story of Saints Joachim and Anna. With a readable and creative style, Nicole animates the account of their barrenness "as an icon of thanksgiving, . . . a transfigured pattern of living we can conform our hearts to however our own journeys through fertility and infertility may end." Those who find themselves in this kind of grief may or may not be able to conceive ultimately, but the roadmap we find in Joachim and Anna's story is applicable and healing to all. Infertility is not the end of the road.

There is so little written on infertility in Orthodoxy, and it continues to be a sensitive and misunderstood issue. At the same time, however, this is not a marginal concern—we have all been touched by the agony of infertility, directly or indirectly, through family, friends, parishioners, coworkers, or acquaintances. *Under the Laurel Tree* rightly recognizes the various forms of this condition as a significant source of grief and marital strain. As such, this book will greatly help not only women but also men better face their grief as individuals and as couples. It also serves as an invaluable resource for anyone seeking to aid and assist these couples.

Through this book we learn by example from a woman who, though fighting intense battles of her own, is also a wellspring of deep serenity. A woman who, with her characteristic warmth, tenderness, and openness, invites us not only to see what is plainly visible to our eyes, but to see as the Lord does, namely "into the heart." In offering her deep personal struggle and a disarming vulnerability, Nicole reminds us how accessible God is and how He can and will help us as He has helped her through the entangled emotions of childlessness.

As such, *Under the Laurel Tree* is a strong and decisive victory for Christ. It is without hesitation or reservation that I highly recommend *Under the Laurel Tree* to everyone, professionals and non-professionals alike.

Albert Rossi, PhD
Director of Counseling and Psychological Services,
Saint Vladimir's Orthodox Seminary
Author of *Becoming a Healing Presence*

Acknowledgments

This is not the kind of book a little girl with authorial ambitions dreams about writing as she grows up. I am grateful for whatever measure my experience can serve to comfort others. Still, I would not have had the bravery or hope to put words to this grief were it not for the help and encouragement of a number of people God has enriched my life with.

First, to my priest and colleague at the Orthodox School of Theology at Trinity College, Rev. Dr. Geoffrey Ready: thank you for allowing your sermon on the Feast of the Nativity of the Theotokos to be co-opted as the premise of this book. Your support of this project has furthered my thinking and helped me tell a new story about childlessness. Thank you also to my confessor, Fr. Steven Kostoff, whom I can always count on for pastoral guidance, deadpan wisdom, and the occasional but well-played Woody Allen quote.

To those who participated in the *Under the Laurel Tree Questionnaire:* thank you immeasurably for sharing your experiences and enriching this book with a community of diverse voices. In the solitude of writing, you reminded me I am not alone in this isolating struggle. And to all others who over the years have shared their experiences of infertility with me, I know who you are and am thankful beyond words to share in this fellowship of suffering and thanksgiving.

I would also like to extend my thanks to folks who provided editorial, inspirational, or conceptual assistance as I was writing. First, to Dr. Al Rossi: your wisdom and encouragement while I was writing this were an immeasurable gift to me. Thank you for your generous willingness in providing feedback on each chapter as they were being written and writing the foreword. I have respected and been helped by your ministry for years; it was a great honor to include your foreword in this book. To Dr. Sarah Bereza, Dr. Susan Dunning, and Laura Jansson for your skilled and perceptive feedback on various drafts of this book, which helped produce a stronger and more resonant final draft. To Elissa Bjeletich, for honest conversations and for lending me your sanity on occasion. To the ladies group at Holy Myrrhbearers Orthodox Church in Toronto for allowing me to test early ideas and excerpts from this book, and to students and colleagues at the Orthodox School of Theology at Trinity College in Toronto for the ways they challenge me to communicate Orthodox ideas clearly and meaningfully. To Presvytera Dr. Jeannie Constantinou for a helpful conversation early in the writing process, and for connecting me with several useful sources, particularly St. John Chrysostom's sermons on Hannah. To John Papadopoulos and all the librarians and staff at the John M. Kelly Library (St. Michael's College) and the John W. Graham Library (Trinity College) at the University of Toronto, whose holdings proved invaluable to this project. To the team at Ancient Faith Publishing, for accepting this publication and helping it become better. And because sometimes one has to get back to one's roots to dig deep, thanks to Chad and Holly Larson for hosting me in Wisconsin while I put the finishing touches on the manuscript.

To countless others who have prayed for me, believed in me, and reminded me to remember God in my struggles and in my writing, I am forever grateful.

Acknowledgments

To the various doctors and specialists my husband and I have worked with over the years: thank you for treating us and others who come your way with respect, sensitivity, and dignity. Your patience, compassion for the human condition, and awareness of mystery have taught me much.

To the Lyon and Roccas families for their unconditional love, support, and understanding over the years.

And finally, to Basil Roccas, my "co-yoker" and the Joachim to my Anna: this book would not have been written without you because it is only with and alongside you I am learning to walk through this grief. I forever treasure the gardens and des(s)erts we have shared along the way. With all my heart, thank you for the gift of sharing this journey together, and trusting me to write about it. Teamwork!

Introduction

[O]n a certain day, Ann[a] arose and went down to her garden and sat beneath one of the laurel trees. As she looked, she noticed a nest there with young and said with a sigh:

Woe is me, miserable person,
that I am not worthy to be like a bird
rejoicing greatly over its young! . . .
I am like a breathless, rootless rock,
incapable to become green or procreate. . . .
To what else shall I compare myself
and in what trinkets shall I find solace in my life?[1]

A SNOWFLAKE IN SEPTEMBER

An icy burst of air greeted me as I trundled up from the subway station in downtown Toronto. It was the beginning of September and the first truly cold day after a long, torrid summer. Pedestrians bustled past, clinging to their frozen grimaces and untimely winter coats. Maybe I would have joined in their bitterness had something not caught my eye first: a lone snowflake falling from heaven to earth. (Did I mention this was September? Welcome to Canada.) No one else appeared to notice, anxious as they were to arrive at their warm destinations. No, this glimmer of white was meant for my eyes only—a gift, an extravagance. A sign. It recalled a simple truth that now seems too fragile or clichéd to render in words: that seasons change; that no matter how long the sun-scorched droughts of faith or famine may last, they will not last forever; that somehow behind and amid all things is a God who is mysteriously, perplexingly good.

I haven't always been like this, wanting or needing nature to remind me of God's benevolence. But over five years of infertility—or childlessness, barrenness, whatever one wishes to call it (no euphemism will ease its sting)—will do that. It will take our expectations for how the world works—and for life, and marriage—and turn them inside out. And in the grief, the struggle will come to be about much more than what is or isn't growing in one's womb. It will touch every facet of life, which we once assumed was a straightforward biological process, but which now appears to be a gaping and vicious, unattainable yet beautiful mystery. And, eventually, we'll have to make a choice. On the one hand, we can either decide to see everything around us as a sign of our emptiness; or we can choose, rather painfully, to see all things as a sign of God's fullness, His presence.

Not that I have mastered this choice, nor am I usually so prone to poetic reflection on crowded city streets. But it was September 8, the Feast of the Nativity of the Theotokos, the day Orthodox and Catholic Christians alike commemorate the birth of the Virgin Mary. Fittingly, it's the first feast of the Orthodox liturgical year, which commences on September 1, marking—as St. Andrew of Crete put it—"the beginning of feasts. It represents the first [boundary] of the [feasts] against the Law and the shadows, yet also the entrance of those [that lead] to grace and truth."[2] Thus this day commemorates not only the beginning of Mary's life but the beginning of salvation. But the thing you also have to know about this date is that it's a veritable High Holy Day for folks dealing with infertility, which—more than any other—was the reason I was on my way to a Liturgy when that snowflake appeared.

According to pious tradition, Mary's parents, Joachim and Anna, struggled for fifty years to conceive a child. As celebratory as it is, the birth of the Mother of God contains within it the haunting undertones of their long-suffering grief. Perhaps more than any other feast of the church year, this is a day that joins the scourge of childlessness with the hope of conception in unbroken thanksgiving. The story of Joachim and Anna—as well as the early life and adulthood of Mary through the birth of Christ—were eventually recorded in the *Protoevangelium of James*, an early Christian text that evokes the startlingly human fabric of Mary's life. Although written in the second century, the *Protoevangelium* would gain greater traction starting in the sixth century, with the rise of Marian feast days.[3]

It was on this text, particularly its first five chapters describing Joachim and Anna's barrenness, that my priest preached his homily on that cold September morning. He recalled that for Joachim and Anna's entire marriage, Anna's womb had remained empty, despite both partners doing "everything right" before God. So dark was their grief that the couple even separated for a time—Joachim fled to the desert to pray and fast, Anna wrote him off as dead (and herself as a widow). Like many couples caught in the clenched jaws of childlessness, their first instinct was to face their pain in isolation, alienating themselves not only from one another but also from their friends and spiritual community.

Rather miraculously, though, they were reunited. They went on to conceive Mary, who in turn would go on to bear Jesus, the Son of God, in an even more miraculous way. But I'm getting ahead of myself.

FRAMES OF FAITH

In his sermon, Fr. Geoffrey compared this story to a reel of film, the kind one might find in an old cinema. Its narrative is composed of numerous frames, a collection of moments that wind past in the storied arc of faith. Stop the reel at any one of the frames—the barrenness, the shame, the separation—and you are left with confusion and despair. By the same token, viewing the frame of Mary's birth apart from the suffering that preceded it would fail to convey the full magnitude of its life-giving significance.

The Christian life as a whole, Fr. Geoffrey explained, is not unlike the journey of Joachim and Anna through childlessness. Along the way, we are frequently tempted to "stop the story," to camp out in one frame or another, becoming fixed in either despair or jubilation, valleys or mountaintops. But the essence of faith, he reckoned, means *not* stopping. It is, instead, the courage to persevere—to keep winding the reel, to keep moving through all the phases of the story God may grant us. Faith is resisting the urge to pitch one's tent in either the depths or the heights, the crucifixions or resurrections, of life. In short, it is the whole path, the willingness to persist through all the saving events of our lives, for as long and as many times as we are given.

Faith means resisting the urge to camp out in one frame or another of our story, becoming fixed in either grief or elation. It is the courage to keep winding the reel, to persist through all the saving events of our lives as long and as many times as we are given.

The more I have reflected on and reread the story of Joachim and Anna, the more it has become a kind of roadmap for me, a travel guide through a grief that once lacked any sense of orientation. In writing this book, I hope to offer that map to others.

Infertility is rarely addressed in a meaningful way within the Church or society at large. We live in a world of convenience, and infertility—with its messy physicality, its unpredictability, its protracted grief—is decidedly *inconvenient*. Life, so our culture increasingly asserts, is supposed to be conceived, lived, and died according to our own terms and temporal specifications. While reproductive medicine has done much to help couples navigate the medical side of infertility, as our own specialist once told us candidly, even the best experts only know something like sixty percent of what there probably is to know about how human life is conceived.

At the end of the day, life is a mystery. And mystery can work many wondrous things, but it first confronts us with the chaos of our own smallness and powerlessness. Perhaps it is for this reason that infertility, in both its spiritual and medical contexts, still feels taboo: do we really want to acknowledge a dimension of reality in which we are small, in which life is not entirely under our sway, in which God's ways aren't fully clear and perhaps never will be?

Mystery can work many wondrous things, but it first confronts us with the chaos of our own smallness and powerlessness. Perhaps it is for this reason that infertility, in both its spiritual and medical contexts, still feels taboo: do we really want to acknowledge a dimension of reality in which we are small, in which life is not entirely under our sway, in which God's ways aren't fully clear and perhaps never will be?

WHY JOACHIM AND ANNA:
THE PROBLEM WITH "JUST REMEMBER SARAH"

Experiencing childlessness in Christian circles, particularly as a woman, drastically increases one's risk of being advised to "just remember Sarah" (or Rachel or Rebecca or Hannah, to name a few of the so-called "barren matriarchs" of the Old Testament). I am sometimes baffled by this advice, well-intentioned though it may be. Somehow between the mandrakes, concubines, desperation, and conniving jealousy, I find it difficult to locate myself in their biographies, especially Sarah's. I suppose the lesson is that God provides, despite human weakness. But on some level, these tales dredge up more infertility baggage than they resolve.

The story of Joachim and Anna differs from Old Testament accounts of childlessness in several ways. First, it is about a couple, not just a woman—and not just two individuals. While we encounter both Joachim and Anna as distinct persons, their marriage—its ebb and flow, its separation and reunification—features almost as a parallel character or storyline. This underscores something we often overlook about infertility: it affects and encompasses the whole marriage. Its grief is not limited to one partner or the other. Tending to our marriages, as much as to our individual pain, is an important component of facing childlessness well.

Second, by Joachim and Anna's time, humanity seems to have come a long way in its salvific encounters with infertility. Gone is the bitter scheming, the extortion, and the bizarre manipulation that always seem to go hand in hand with barrenness, at least in the Genesis accounts. Gone, too, are the "alternate routes" to progeny via concubines, maidservants, and multiple wives. Like Elizabeth and Zechariah, who would conceive St. John the Baptist a generation later, Joachim and Anna were born into a time and place where monogamous marriage was the expectation. In an environment where virtually the only way around childlessness was divorce or death, the tragedy of infertility is crystallized in Joachim and Anna's plight. Without a release valve, the swell of emotion and near marital breakdown, while heartbreaking, lends an unusually authentic feel to such an ancient story. (This element of their narrative is also one that speaks poignantly to childless couples of today, who must weigh their grief against new "alternate routes" around infertility, such as surrogacy and gamete or embryo donation.)

Finally, Joachim and Anna just seem like *real people*. Not that Sarah and her successors weren't, but something about their story makes it unusually accessible and authentic. Whether that's because of the narrative conventions of the genre or the literary flair of the text's author (who, despite the title of the text, wasn't actually James—more on this and other aspects of the *Protoevangelium* in Chapter 3), by the end of this story, Anna and Joachim become more than just a couple of saints; they come to be people you would want to sit down and have coffee with. You want to ask how they did it— how they managed to keep praying through it all, how they found it within themselves to keep turning to God and to one another. In short, they become fellow travelers, co-sufferers. They get it.

Somehow between the mandrakes, concubines, desperation, and conniving jealousy, I find it difficult to locate myself in the biographies of the barren matriarchs of the Old Testament, especially Sarah's. I suppose the lesson in her story is that God provides, despite human weakness. But on some level, these tales dredge up more infertility baggage than they resolve.

FIVE STAGES OF INFERTILITY GRIEF

The Five Stages of Grief according to Elizabeth Kübler-Ross	The Five Stages of Infertility Grief in the story of Joachim and Anna
Denial	Shame (Chapter 4)
Anger	Separation (Chapter 5)
Bargaining	Anger (Chapter 6)
Depression	Bargaining (Chapter 7)
Acceptance	Thanksgiving (Chapter 8)

Figure 1: Reimagining the Five Stages of Grief for Infertility

Returning to Fr. Geoffrey's "film frames" of faith, I can't help but think of the five stages of grief famously mapped out in the late 1960s by Elizabeth Kübler-Ross to account for the ways terminally ill patients come to terms with their mortality. Many have memorized them using the popular "DABDA" acronym: denial, anger, bargaining, depression, acceptance (see Figure 1). While no "stage theory" can fully demystify the great enigma of human sorrow, models like this serve as a basic map, a locating mechanism in an otherwise disorienting emotional landscape.

We don't often recognize infertility as a true loss, largely because it revolves around something we may never have had in the first place. Normally, we mourn the loss of things or people who were once in our lives, however briefly. But in infertility, the ordinary substance and sequence of grief are undone—we mourn not that which *has* happened and changed us, but that which *hasn't*, yet has changed us all the same. It is, one might say, an *apophatic* grief, a grief of negation. In theology, the apophatic approach insists we can never fully articulate who God *is*; we can only apprehend Him through what we know He is not. When we do this, when we carve away all that God is not, the shape of Him emerges, as though "through a glass darkly" (1 Cor. 13:12, KJV)—holy, inscrutable, ineffable. The mystery of infertility is a little like this. By rational standards, we have (literally) nothing to grieve. But over time, all the gaps and negative spaces of childlessness reveal a shape, a figure, a whisper of a life we long to hold in our arms.

Infertility is an apophatic grief. By rational standards, we have (literally) nothing to grieve. But over time, all the gaps and negative spaces of childlessness reveal a shape, a figure, a whisper of a life we long to hold in our arms.

And so infertility prompts an emotional sojourn not unlike any other kind of grief. The stages of this special grief are uniquely borne out in the story of Joachim and Anna. In my reading of the text, the ones that jumped out at me were shame, separation, anger, bargaining, and thanksgiving (see Figure 1), each of which serves as the basis for a chapter in Part II of this book. While some of these stages align with Kübler-Ross's famous model, however, there are important differences. Missing are denial and despair, for example—not because they never feature in childlessness, but because I sought to highlight the unique ways Anna and Joachim faced their grief. In place of denial and despair are shame and separation, which feature prominently in their story. Shame and separation, as forces of grief, threaten to disintegrate rather than reintegrate husbands and wives, and they require careful and sensitive attention. The final stage, for our purposes, is not the "acceptance" of Kübler-Ross's model but thanksgiving. Anna and Joachim's journey ends in a place that goes beyond passive resignation and culminates in active, abundant gratitude.

One last note: This grouping is intended only as a provisional, heuristic framework—driven, admittedly, by personal perceptions as much as (or even more than) true textual analysis—and is not a definitive statement about infertility grief as a clinical phenomenon. (Indeed, experts illuminate different stages of infertility grief than I do.)[4] Still, I have done my best to bridge insights from a host of different areas—theology, homiletics, and scientific research, to name a few—with the lived experience of childlessness in order to say something meaningful and life-giving about the complicated, soul-wrenching reality of infertility grief.

HOW TO READ THIS BOOK

Under the Laurel Tree is crafted with versatility in mind; read it in a way that will most benefit you. It begins with three introductory chapters (Part I) that define infertility, contextualize it in the Orthodox Church, and introduce readers to Joachim and Anna. Part II—the body of this book—is devoted to the stages of grief described above, the frames of faith that comprise Joachim and Anna's journey through childlessness. They proceed chronologically through the first five chapters of the *Protoevangelium*, each one focusing on a consecutive "frame" or stage of Anna and Joachim's grief: shame (Chapter 4); separation (Chapter 5); anger (Chapter 6); bargaining (Chapter 7); and, finally, thanksgiving and reconciliation (Chapter 8).

The book concludes with an epilogue about blamelessness. Here we return, with Joachim, to the temple, where his shame began, now with a child on the horizon. In bringing his thank offerings, Joachim re-encounters his own blamelessness before God, a reminder that what lies even deeper than our desire for children is the assurance of salvation and the love of God.

In addition, several appendices in the back of this book provide practical guidance for those in ministry or wishing to learn more about the key topics that surfaced in this book.

While I welcome you to read this book in whatever order is most helpful, here are three suggested reading plans for the main audiences of this book:

For individuals or couples acutely struggling with infertility grief: I recommend skipping ahead and reading Chapters 4–8 and the Epilogue. Afterward, going back to Chapters 1–3 will give you a better idea of the context and significance of what you've read. If you are reading this together as a couple, the questions at the end of each chapter can be used to foster discussion and reflection.

For priests, seminarians, parishioners, or loved ones seeking to better support childless couples: Read Appendix II first, then the chapters of the book in sequential order, paying special attention to the context Chapter 2 establishes. The discussion questions for each chapter may be useful for parish studies or support groups.

For physicians or mental health practitioners who may or may not be Orthodox, but who wish to better help their Orthodox patients and clients: Begin by reading Chapters 1–2 and the appendices. This gives a better understanding of the unique challenges Orthodox couples with infertility face, resources that may benefit them, and which remaining portions of the book will be most valuable for those you serve.

Throughout this book, I have supplemented my own writing and reflections with callouts from others who have been in the trenches of infertility. My hope is to lend a sense of community to what is otherwise a lonely journey. I am immensely grateful to all who shared their experiences in the *Under the Laurel Tree Questionnaire*, which I circulated online while writing this book. One of my favorite ways to "read" this book is by simply flipping through the pages and perusing their words—they are powerful reminders that I am not alone, even when surrounded by a grief that too often remains hidden and silent.

This book is not (just) for women, mainly because women aren't the only side of the gene pool grieving infertility. Men are uniquely sensitive to the shame of a childless marriage. Yet, in both Church and society, we feminize infertility and its grief in subtle ways. Not only does this harm women, men, and their marriages, it perpetuates a depiction of men as unwilling or emotionally inept father figures.

WHAT THIS BOOK IS NOT

Now that I've highlighted what this book is, it's time to talk about what it is not.

First, *Under the Laurel Tree* is not (just) for women, mainly because women aren't the only side of the gene pool grieving infertility. The narrative of Joachim and Anna is a jarring reminder that men are uniquely sensitive to the shame of a childless marriage. Yet, in both Church and society, we feminize infertility and its grief in subtle ways. We speak in hushed tones about a "barren womb" and assume either that the "problem" lies with the woman or that females are naturally more upset about a lack of children than their husbands. Not only does this harm women, men, and their marriages, it perpetuates a depiction of men as unwilling or emotionally inept father figures. For this reason, although I experience infertility as a woman and speak from that point of view in this book, I seek to do so in ways that integrate rather than denigrate men. This was not entirely easy; on the whole, I found that while women were eager to articulate their grief with me, men were more reticent to go on record, even those who expressed deep anguish in more casual settings, and even when anonymity was guaranteed. This ambivalence, I believe, testifies to the depth of shame that surrounds male infertility, particularly in a society that affords men few acceptable avenues to express vulnerability.

Second, this book does not romanticize or minimize infertility. Not everyone gets a happy ending; neither does this grief automatically subside when a couple pursues adoption. As a church, we must recognize that infertility rates are rising around the world (more on that in Chapter 1), and this translates to increasing numbers of couples in our pews who are suffering deeply (though often silently). To begin bearing one another's burdens in the midst of this tragedy, we must acknowledge that infertility is not a "little thing" but a major loss that can affect how a person views and experiences all of life. But as difficult as it is, many can benefit from medical and therapeutic intervention—a reality we sometimes shy away from in the Church. Along with prayer, prayer, and more prayer, couples (both wives and husbands) should be encouraged to see a doctor whenever pregnancy is proving difficult to achieve or maintain, and a counselor or other marriage professional when their marriage experiences undue stress as a result.

Third, this book is not about bioethics. Much has been written for Orthodox audiences about infertility from the perspective of biomedical concerns, reproductive technology, and the sanctity of human life (see Appendix II for further resources on this and other key topics from this book). Sorely lacking, however, is a focused and sensitive discussion about the emotional aspects of infertility grief and their impact on the marital relationship. This, to me at least, is actually a more primary issue. As with so many other wounds in life, we can only decide what to "do" about infertility once we have begun to grieve well. Gradually operating outside the shame, isolation, and deep sadness of this loss empowers people to explore their options for the future with greater intention and resilience. *Under the Laurel Tree* addresses infertility first and foremost as a source of grief, not a bioethical dilemma to be resolved. I'm not here to give advice, to tell you what you should or shouldn't do, or to inquire whether you've tried this diet or that doctor, but to remind you it's okay to be *here*. It's okay to take a break from the timing and tests, advice and ethical questions, and to just be in this moment God has given us, in all its turmoil and apparent meaninglessness.

Finally, this book does not end with a baby. I'm not going to accompany readers through this journey of grief only to throw a sucker punch in the epilogue about how I "accidentally" got a miracle pregnancy while writing this book. (Although, God, if you're listening—that *would* make a good story to tell the grandkids I'd like to have someday . . .) Jokes aside, books like that always feel like a bit of a betrayal. Just when the author has gained my trust and camaraderie, she blindsides me with her good fortune, churning up the same isolation and grief that led me to the book in the first place.

This is partly why (spoiler alert) *Under the Laurel Tree* doesn't even end with Anna's pregnancy. It concludes a few "frames" before Mary enters the world, at a moment in time when Anna and Joachim find it within themselves to reconcile as a couple and give thanks to God. Yes, Anna's pregnancy has been foretold, and the Conception of the Theotokos is imminent. But just because someone receives good news does not mean she or he will welcome it gladly. The older brother of the prodigal son certainly didn't. And, I hate to bring this up again, but just remember Sarah—when she was told that she would conceive, she laughed at God (Gen. 18:12), later denying it—this was not a shriek of joy but an eruption of contempt that had been building for quite some time.

But let's not judge Sarah too harshly—we've all been there. At the very least, her story is a sobering reminder that gratitude does not happen automatically. For Joachim and Anna, it was ultimately a choice, one they had to have made long in advance, perhaps in the early days of their grief. That they could still *fathom* God's goodness, let alone respond to it with the open arms of thanksgiving, indicates that they had managed to cut a different, less bitter path through their anguish all along.

Just because someone receives good news does not mean she or he will welcome it gladly. That Joachim and Anna could still fathom God's goodness, let alone respond to it with the open arms of thanksgiving, indicates that they had managed to cut a different, less bitter path through their anguish all along.

A FINAL NOTE ON THANKSGIVING

As flimsy a consolation as gratitude may feel sometimes, it's one thing—perhaps the only thing—we truly have control over in this struggle. Reconnecting with and exercising our God-given free will, I believe, is an essential part of the grieving process. When struggling to get pregnant, it can feel like the whole world is out of whack, that we're merely a pawn in some deterministic game of biological chance. I'm not ending with Joachim and Anna's thank offerings because it's elegant or just sounds Christian, but because I truly believe that, however agonizing, giving thanks is *the* goal, *the* pinnacle of a well-lived life, and not just for people dealing with infertility. It is the crowning glory of the responsive, eucharistic mode of being we are called to in Christ.

As an icon of that thanksgiving, Joachim and Anna's story offers a transfigured pattern of living we can conform our hearts to however our own journeys through fertility and infertility may end. Wherever we go from here, it affords a way to fill and redeem our time on this earth during what often feels like a vacuous waiting game. As desperately as we may want children (and as holy and healthy as that desire is), our happiness and sense of freedom in this life need not depend on that outcome. If they do, we risk setting ourselves up for a bitterness that not even a "quiver full of children" (Psalm 127:4, NKJV) will be able to soften. "For what profit is it to a man if he gains the whole world, and loses his own soul?" Jesus once asked His disciples (Matt. 16:26). Similarly, as I have asked myself on many painful occasions, what good is it to gain children but lose my capacity for hope, for thanksgiving, and for God Himself?

In Orthodoxy, it is tempting to speak of saints as distant figures who were somehow above the pain of earthly struggle. What is perhaps most encouraging about the story of Joachim and Anna is that they very clearly weren't. Even these righteous figures, often referred to as the "ancestors of God" because of their blood relation to the Incarnate Christ, did not pass through the valley of childlessness unscathed. They grieved and lamented deeply, until they had nothing left to bargain with or offer to God except their barely willing spirits. Yet, just when they had least reason to trust in God's graciousness, they wound the reel one frame further, as Fr. Geoffrey would say. And in doing so, they received something far greater than what they had imagined or prayed for: not (merely) a pregnancy or a renewed marriage or a happy ending, but salvation itself.

PART I

Understanding Infertility

CHAPTER I

What Is Infertility?

Infertility is one of those things you assume you understand until you actually experience it. For much of my young adulthood, I shrugged it off as an abstract medical term that afflicts others—it's "just" when someone can't get pregnant. "Just" because, as I reasoned then, there are surely worse things in life. Cancer. Death. The threat of nuclear war. I knew a few childless couples before I got married and, although I could empathize with them to a degree, I occasionally wondered why they were *so* upset. Couldn't they just adopt?

It's not until the reality of childlessness invades your own life, marriage, and hopes for the future (some of which you never knew were so important to you) that you begin to glimpse what Bethany, in her response to the *Under the Laurel Tree Questionnaire* I circulated while writing this book, described as the "stabbing, biting, clawing monster" of infertility grief. And yes, there are worse things in life, but at least those things are, well, *things*. In so many ways infertility is the absence of a thing. The absence of a child, yes, but also the absence of parenthood, of getting to see your spouse as a mother or father, of getting to fulfill certain social roles you assumed were a given—and these are just the "things" that can be articulated in words.

To start giving shape to this intangible grief, we need to begin with its physical source. What is infertility? What causes it? In answering these questions, I draw on basic medical understandings. One might be tempted to view this chapter as perfunctory—a way to get the "medical stuff" out of the way so we could move on to the "real stuff," namely the emotional and theological dimensions of infertility. But the medical and physical contours of our experience are tied to theology and faith in ways we can't (and shouldn't) untangle. Christians worship a God who sent His Incarnate Son into the world of flesh and physicality to redeem, elevate, and affirm the dignity of our bodily existence. "The incarnation itself," writes Orthodox physician Daniel Hinshaw, "should liberate the believing Christian from . . . ambivalence regarding healing, since Christ made it possible that great healing can come by means of the tangible, whether it be in the consecrated Bread and Wine or the *touch* (e.g., medications, massage, surgery) of a healer/physician received in the context of faith and prayer."[5]

Nonetheless, there are many arenas in which body and soul, flesh and spirit, continue to be at odds with one another—and infertility is one of them. Something about this condition, as distinct from many other physical maladies, evokes a troubling anti-medical bias in Orthodox circles. Perhaps this stems from a view of medicine as antithetical to faith and genuine prayer, or perhaps, in our reticence towards the bioethical questions that surround assisted reproduction, we overcompensate by shunning medical consultation altogether.

Whatever the case, despite the best intentions, many childless people in the Church have been negatively affected by this bias. Some have been explicitly advised by well-meaning loved ones to "just pray" for a child instead of seeing a doctor, only to question or regret this choice later in life when it is too late for medical counsel to do any good. Others who have sought medical advice have been judged or criticized by priests, fellow parishioners, or Orthodox family members for doing so, in some cases causing irreparable harm to their relationship with the Church and their faith. To be clear, I am not (only) talking about couples who opt for controversial procedures like IVF—I'm also referring to people who consult a physician *at all* for their infertility.

It is not my intention to give advice, nor do I wish to imply that couples must unequivocally take one particular path through their infertility, medical or otherwise. But as my own priest once said when my husband and I were weighing some of these questions for ourselves, whatever decisions we make when it comes to infertility, we must make them with all the prayers *and* all the information we can muster. With God as our strength, we must discern not only *what* our decisions will be but *why*. In doing so, we will not only guard against undue regret but also ensure we are able to continue approaching God with faith and love rather than with a troubled conscience or resentful heart. As important as prayer and pastoral counsel are in this process (we'll address these aspects of infertility in Chapter 2), they must be integrated with the physical reality of our bodies and the possibilities medicine affords if we are to live our faith as whole, soul-enfleshed creatures.

∞

"After two years of trying, I needed numbers, facts— anything more concrete or palpable than 'God's will.' I told my husband I desperately needed him to be willing to go through necessary diagnostics to see if either of us was just not capable of creating a healthy child. For a while he fought back on this and when I asked why, he finally explained he was scared he was the reason we couldn't conceive." —Sophia

DEFINING INFERTILITY

For the purpose of this book, infertility is understood in the clinical sense: *a couple's failure to achieve a pregnancy (or bring a pregnancy to full term) after 12 months of unprotected sex.* It can result from female, male, or unexplained factors, or all of the above (see Figure 2 below for a summary of these and other terms). Most experts recommend couples see their primary care provider if conception doesn't occur within one year (or six months if the woman is over age 35).

Falling outside of this umbrella definition are several modes of infertility that are often overlooked. Secondary infertility, for example, occurs when a couple who already has a child is unable to conceive a second (or third, or fourth) one. Couples in this category face a painful and often overlooked dimension of infertility. A friend of mine who was never able to have a second child once told me she rarely talks about her grief, though it's something she struggles with every day. She's too afraid that expressing her sadness will imply she's not thankful for her now teenaged son. Although my own experience is with primary infertility, and much of the book will reflect this, I have included voices and examples from folks dealing with secondary infertility as well.

⬭

"*I often felt tremendous condemnation for wanting another child. How ungrateful was I to God for being so greedy to want another baby when I should just be thankful for the one He gave me?*" —Bethany

⬭

Multiple miscarriages are another form of infertility, one that carries its own special grief. For some couples, the challenge is not *getting* but *staying* pregnant. For them, infertility brings two parallel griefs: being (as yet) unable to bring children into the world outside the womb, and mourning the life (or lives) lost to miscarriage. Although pregnancy loss overlaps with infertility grief on many points, this book is intentionally focused on the latter to avoid shortchanging the unique anguish of miscarriage. Still, I hope this broader conversation will, in some way, touch the pain of miscarriage and allow those who have endured multiple pregnancy losses to find solace in these pages.

A final mode of infertility that has gained attention only recently is what some have termed situational or social infertility, in which childlessness is the result of circumstantial rather than physical factors.[6] This occurs, for instance, when couples marry later in life, or when an all-consuming illness or major life stressor precludes them from trying to conceive during their childbearing years. I know several couples of whom one spouse was diagnosed with cancer while they were trying to start a family. Although the cancer didn't necessarily damage their fertility in a biological sense, it understandably forced them to put their desire for children on hold long enough that it effectively prevented the conception of biological children.

Situational infertility may also be a way for singles to acknowledge their infertility grief; along with desiring a spouse, many singles also long for children *with* that spouse. The point to remember is that although situational infertility is not medical or biological in origin—indeed the individual or couple may be perfectly "fertile," biologically—it is not necessarily a more mild grief. Often, it is marked by an intense sense of regret or bitterness over lost time and irretrievable opportunities.

BASIC TERMS AND DEFINITIONS

» **Infertility** is defined as the failure to achieve or sustain a pregnancy after 12 or more months of unprotected sexual intercourse.

» **Primary infertility** occurs when a woman trying to conceive has never been able to get pregnant or carry a pregnancy to full term.

» **Secondary infertility** is the inability to achieve or carry a pregnancy to full term after having one or more children in the past.

» **Situational infertility** happens when childlessness is the result of circumstantial rather than biological factors, such as singleness or marrying late in life.

» **Male factor infertility** refers to the presence of abnormal semen parameters or ejaculatory function in male partners of couples who have been unable to conceive naturally within 12 months of unprotected sex.

» **Female factor infertility** can be caused by ovulation disorders, scarred or damaged fallopian tubes, pelvic inflammatory disease, anatomical abnormalities in the uterus or cervix, or endometriosis, a condition in which extra uterine tissue grows outside the uterus and can disrupt fertility in a variety of ways.

» **Unexplained infertility** is diagnosed when the cause of a couple's infertility remains unknown, even after a full medical workup of both partners.

» **Sterility** is the inability to conceive or produce life at all, due to a known reason (e.g. absence of a uterus).

Sources

"Female Infertility," *Mayo Clinic* website (https://www.mayoclinic.org/diseases-conditions/female-infertility/symptoms-causes/syc-20354308).

"Infertility definitions and terminology," *World Health Organization* website (https://www.who.int/reproductivehealth/topics/infertility/definitions/en/).

"Male infertility," *Mayo Clinic* website

DIAGNOSED INFERTILITY AS MYSTERY

Although I don't have any statistical proof, I'd wager that fertility specialists use words like "mystery" and "inexplicable" more than other physicians. Even in the medical arena of infertility, there tend to be more questions and profundities than answers. I have occasionally (okay, constantly) cornered our doctor and demanded he tell us once and for all whether we'll get pregnant naturally—I like to have a plan. "I can't tell you that," he'll reply, barely disguising his eye roll. "No one can. At the end of the day, conception is a mystery." So says one of the most successful practitioners of his kind in all of Canada.

The elusive aspect of infertility makes it unique among other medical conditions—it is not actually a diagnosis, at least not in the formal sense. It's much more the acknowledgment of a mystery, the ageless enigma of two people unable to conceive for reasons yet unknown. After tests and screenings, that mystery may solidify into a more specific diagnosis—endometriosis, polycystic ovarian syndrome (PCOS), and low sperm count are some of the most common causes of infertility. These may or may not respond to treatment, thus leading a couple down ever-unfolding paths as the permutations of their particular circumstances reveal themselves. But even when there are answers and medical options, there will always be something mysterious—something tenuous and hidden—about this whole sojourn until one either gets pregnant or exceeds her childbearing years. And even then . . . I think, even if one day I am blessed with a pregnancy, I will always look back on this season of my life and wonder at it all, not just with sadness but also with an awe-filled acknowledgment of all that remained unseen and unfathomed.

"*Fertility is understood as a 'given' in society. So many women talk about planning their pregnancies and deciding which month would be better for birth. I would have given so much just to get pregnant, regardless of the timing."* —Lorna

It's hard to dwell in uncertainty for this long—it's like being stuck in the penultimate chord of a symphony for years, waiting for the conductor to wave in the final strike to resolve the dissonance. But as hard as the ambiguity may be, what I've come to value about mystery is that it is malleable. Soft. Like a piece of pottery whose clay never fully dries, mystery and our understandings of it are always unfolding, always changing. This comforts some hidden place within me, maybe because it means the door will never fully close. Even if I pass beyond my childbearing years, it seems as though mystery, if I let it, will carry me to the next good thing—not a biological life inside me, perhaps, but something.

I don't know what your diagnosis is or what options your physician has recommended to you. Much less do I know whether you (or I) will ever get pregnant. But I do know we have a responsibility, as human beings, to face and bear witness to the mystery of infertility. When people tell of the first time they saw their baby, they struggle to convey the sheer awe they felt. Who doesn't marvel at the wondrous sight of an infant, all writhing fingers and toes in miniature? But this is only one view of the great picture of life—the recognizable, front side of the tapestry of humanity that is ultimately not ours to weave. In infertility, we are invited to walk around back to peer at that same mystery from the other side. As we do, we glimpse something of the shadows, the loose and dead ends, the gaps and empty spots of human biology and existence. This is hardly a lesser mystery.

Speaking of mysteries, infertility is perhaps the only medical diagnosis given to *two* people (a couple), not just one. It's not that you and your partner happen to have the same condition at the same time, it's that you *share* the same diagnosis—the same medical case. Just as it takes two to tango when making a baby, it takes two to *not* make one. This reality trickles down even to the methodological choices many physicians who treat fertility make. Early in our journey through all this, my husband and I were sitting in a consultation room with the couple's fertility specialist we see, scheduling a slew of upcoming appointments. We would both have to go in for several rounds of tests, and after each one the doctor wanted to meet to go over results.

"Can we just trade off so that only one of us has to come to these consultations at a time? We'll keep each other in the loop," I said, thinking of how much personal leave we'd already used up for these daytime appointments.

Our physician stared at me for what felt like a long time.

"Well, are you both trying to get pregnant?" he asked. I nodded.

"And does it take a man *and* a woman to conceive?" I nodded again, this time more hesitantly. I *thought* that's how babies were made.

"Then I expect both of you at these appointments," he informed me.

Thanks a lot, I thought with a scowl. *There goes our vacation time this year.*

I now have more appreciation for his approach. It reminded me that infertility is not just "*my* thing" simply because it is my womb that isn't getting pregnant. Nor does it suddenly switch to my husband's thing when I have a busy schedule and don't want to make time for the consultations. I've witnessed a lot of wedding sermons, but—whatever his beliefs—our physician's admonishment taught me what it really means to be united in one flesh to my husband.

Infertility has many downsides, but one strangely cool perk is getting to share a doctor and medical condition with your spouse.

☙

"Infertility is painful and hard, and even if you have many children, you can still feel the pain of ones you've lost or ones your heart desires." —Eva

☙

REIMAGINING STERILITY

In the section above, I drew attention to the mysterious quality of infertility as a medical diagnosis. There are times, however, when infertility reveals a condition that—in the hardest way—leaves no room for mystery, namely in cases of sterility. Medically, to be sterile means to be unable to produce offspring. (This may occur, for example, if a woman has had her uterus removed due to cancer, or a man has a genetic condition in which his body does not produce sperm.) Sterility is a *predictive* and terminal diagnosis—bearing children will be impossible, regardless of any medical intervention. (By contrast, infertility is more of a *descriptive* and indeterminate diagnosis—it is saying that until now, the couple has been unable to conceive, regardless of what may happen in the future.) While being diagnosed with sterility is relatively rare, there are nonetheless couples out there who face this trauma, and their special grief—as a subset of infertility grief—warrants acknowledgment. It is one thing to realize you *may* never have a child naturally; it is indeed harder to learn that you (and consequently your spouse) *will* never do so.

In this book, I refrain from using the term *sterility* as a synonym for infertility (which I tend to use interchangeably with the words *barrenness* and *childlessness*). My intention here is to honor rather than overlook the presence of sterile people in the conversation on infertility grief, and also to advocate for greater precision and awareness in our language surrounding childlessness. In today's English, sterility has a specific meaning; it is not simply an extreme or hyperbolized way to refer to infertility.

Problematically, one encounters "sterility" in English translations of historical or patristic-era texts where "barrenness" or "childlessness" may have been a better choice—for example when St. Andrew of Crete describes the grief of "sterile" Anna as being "pricked daily by the goads of sterility."[7] It's just my opinion, but I wonder whether the vocabulary of sterility is really the most helpful way to render into English the plight of Anna (not to mention other barren matriarchs of our Tradition). In the first millennium, the Greek word *steira* could refer to an animal that has not brought forth young, a woman who is past childbearing age, or a woman who is barren.[8] Although our English word "sterile" indirectly derives from this root, today an added meaning can be found in virtually any dictionary entry under this word, namely the quality of being "inhospitable" to or "incapable of producing" life. This expansion on traditional notions of sterility, while subtle, is not only harsh but also imprecise when applied to many biblical and extrabiblical contexts. That Anna and her predecessors eventually conceived, however miraculously, demonstrates that they were not actually sterile.

⊗

"*It's difficult to explain to others how I can grieve so hard for someone (a child) I haven't actually met. In so many ways, this loss is a mystery.*" —Vera

⊗

I suppose my real point here, and the underlying reason I avoid the term *sterility* except in direct quotation, is that I don't regard any human being as truly incapable of bearing or producing life—even people who have been medically diagnosed as such. The witness of Christ demonstrates that biological procreation is merely a shadow or icon of the Life He has given us. Our task, whether barren or sterile or fertile, is to manifest that Life to the world through whatever means, opportunities, bodies, and talents He has given us. We bring life into the world every time we are kind, every time we hope in God's mercy, every time we offer ourselves to Him and our neighbor self-sacrificially, every time we do something that creatively and newly manifests Christ to the world. Sterility may be your own medical diagnosis, but it needn't be your spiritual and vocational one. Remembering the diverse ways life can be brought forth in this world gives infertile and even biologically sterile couples an incredible freedom, one that invites them to operate outside shame, social expectations, and stigma.

"*Infertility has made me realize there are other amazing contributions I can make to my church, family, work, and community. I started contemplating being an educator or advocate to women in some way. I also realized I could still be a godmother, and provide spiritual guidance that way. Honestly, it was God's way of getting a very stubborn and headstrong woman to proclaim, 'Thy will be done! I am your servant to use as you will, Lord.'"* —Sophia

DISPELLING MYTHS: FIVE COMMON ASSUMPTIONS ABOUT INFERTILITY AND INFERTILITY GRIEF

In my interactions with others on this subject, a few common assumptions about infertility surface frequently. Since these tend to fall through the cracks of bigger discussions, I have chosen to list them below with brief responses.

MYTH 1: With modern technological and medical advancements, infertility is not as pervasive as it used to be.

Infertility rates are on the rise across the globe, so much so that the World Health Organization has recognized it as a global public health issue. Changing demographic trends (such as the tendency for today's couples to postpone childbearing) only account for a limited percentage of this growing problem. Perhaps the most troubling facet of this tendency, and one experts have yet to explain, is the fact that sperm counts, particularly among Western men, have decreased by roughly fifty percent over the last forty years.[9]

Although assisted reproductive technologies may help infertile couples get pregnant, they do not necessarily treat the underlying causes of infertility. "Something is very wrong with the way we live," said Dr. Hagai Levine, in a May 2018 article for *Today's Parent*. "It's amazing that so many people can't conceive naturally—it's really something we should pay attention to."[10] Rising infertility rates should be on our radar in the Church, particularly for people serving in ministry. They mean that a greater number of couples in our flocks are or will be struggling with childlessness than we might typically assume. Now more than ever, it is vital we learn to speak (or rather, to listen) with love and sensitivity on this issue.

MYTH 2: Infertility is caused by stress.

Like most things in life, the relationship between stress and fertility is more complex than the media, Hollywood, and some insistent mothers-in-law make it out to be. The short answer is that stress is unlikely to be the sole factor behind a couple's infertility. The longer and more complex answer is that the research on this issue is mixed—some studies do suggest stress can delay or postpone conception in *some* (I repeat: *some*) couples, but other studies have failed to replicate this finding. Likewise, some researchers have determined that stress-reduction techniques (acupuncture and massage therapy have the most evidence-backed support) may help certain couples get pregnant who were unable to do so previously. When you add up all the evidence, however, the blatant claim that infertility is caused by stress is an oversimplification at best.

A more certain claim is that infertility itself *causes* stress (as does nagging people to "just relax!"). For some, infertility and its related stressors are enough to trigger full-blown depression, anxiety, or other legitimate mental health struggles. Part of integrating the medical reality of infertility with the totality of our faith means recognizing the impact childlessness can have on our psychological well-being and seeking both pastoral and therapeutic help when necessary.

✺

"*My husband and I have both been diagnosed with depression since finding out about the infertility. It's a double whammy since according to my doctor, depression can hinder efforts to conceive even further. The prayers and rituals of the Church have helped, as has finding physicians who are compassionate and willing to help us address both depression and infertility in ways that are medically and spiritually sound."* —Kira

MYTH 3: In the grand scheme of things, infertility is not that big a deal.

Infertility *is* a big deal for the many couples who experience it. There is evidence to suggest that for women, childlessness ranks among the most painful sources of grief in their lives. (I suspect it is equally difficult for male partners of infertile couples, but there simply isn't enough research on their emotional experiences of infertility to be sure; see Myth 5 below.) Today, we've somehow forgotten how heavy a burden childlessness can be. Once upon a time, we knew, instinctively, that it was one of the saddest things that could happen to a young couple, so much so that laws and stigmas and dogmas were enacted to keep it at a distance. Admittedly, some of these were rather extreme and unloving, but today we've almost gone to the opposite extreme of being so blasé we can barely be bothered to care at all about infertility. After all, women can work and have a livelihood outside of childbearing now, so why are they so upset? In this way, infertility grief often constitutes a form of what social scientists have labeled "disenfranchised grief," grief that is not acknowledged or legitimized by society. As I will repeat a few times over the course of this book, today it is not so much infertility that is stigmatized but the *grief* of infertility that remains taboo.

MYTH 4: Adoption resolves infertility grief.

If nothing works out in the end, there's always adoption, right? I never quite know how to respond to that comment. As beautiful as adoption can be, it is not a "cure" for infertility or the grief that so often accompanies it. I know many couples who eventually adopted after being unable to conceive. They love their adopted child fiercely, but deep down they still grieve the absence of biological children and the childbearing experience.

For all sorts of ethical and emotional reasons, infertility and adoption should be two separate conversations. Adoption is a big deal. It's complicated, time-consuming, in some cases expensive, and it entails a whole other journey of waiting, risk, marital strain, and possible disappointment. A couple has to be prepared for that, which is less likely to happen if they envision adoption merely as the long-awaited promised land to their barren desert. More than this, children—biological or adoptive—should not be regarded as merely the means to our emotional fulfillment as potential parents. When we tell infertile people that they can "just adopt," we imply that the needs/wishes of us adults are the priority—as long as kids are procured in the end, it's all good. I think we can agree that's not exactly the best mentality with which to embark on a path to parenthood.

To guard against this temptation, we have to allow ourselves and the childless couples among us to grapple with adoption on their own terms and in their own time. Some may be unable even to consider adoption until they have exhausted every means of conceiving. They may also need to take some (or a lot of) time to grieve and really say goodbye to their own efforts to conceive. When couples like this embark on the adoption process, they may wish to imagine it as an entirely new and different adventure, a fresh start, rather than a continuation of their infertility story. At the same time, others may thrive in the emotional complexity of still trying to conceive while also starting the early stages of the adoption process. For them, adoption and infertility may be experienced in the same spirit of openness and possibility, two intertwined paths toward whatever awaits them. Still others may decide that despite their deep desire for children, adoption simply isn't something they are able to pursue. That's okay, too.

There is no single or "correct" way to bridge infertility with adoption.

∞

"My husband and I both came from large families, and we were expecting the same for our lives together. When it took so long to get pregnant, I grieved my dream of having a noisy and busy home like the one I grew up in." —Teresa

∞

MYTH 5: Women get more upset about infertility than men.
Ancient paradigms and contemporary depictions both tend toward the assumption that women are more afflicted and emotionally distraught by infertility than men are. Until recently, male experiences of infertility were a black box, an untold story. Even scientific research has largely neglected the male side of infertility grief. And this blind spot extends even into casual conversation. One man, in a study I read that gauged men's emotional reactions to infertility and treatment, anonymously recalled how "everyone asked (quite rightly) how dearest wife was feeling, yet barely a few asked how I was, not even my own mom! Don't they realize it affects us too?"[11] Aaron, a respondent to the *Under the Laurel Tree Questionnaire*, wrote that "men experience infertility silently, but would like to talk about it with other men. There is a stigma to almost any male mental health issue. We are generally okay for women to have issues, but don't like to talk about our own."

The more I talk to men on this subject and read the few male-authored memoirs of infertility on the market, the more I've come to realize that childless men are deeply affected by infertility. Their experiences evade detection, sometimes even by themselves, in part because they are socialized to express (or not express) emotions differently than women. The sooner we begin incorporating their experiences into common perceptions of this struggle, the sooner we will help couples face their grief in a more mutually supportive, maritally satisfying way.[12]

⬥

"*Men experience infertility silently, but would like to talk about it with other men. There is a stigma to almost any male mental health issue. We are generally okay for women to have issues, but don't like to talk about our own.*" —Aaron

⬥

CONCLUSION

In this chapter we have outlined the basic medical understandings of infertility and countered a handful of the most pervasive myths about childlessness in our society. In the Church, we often have a tendency to gloss over the medical particularities of human infirmity in our efforts to promote and prioritize faith. But the supposed dichotomy between medicine and faith is a false one. In the case of infertility, as elsewhere, learning to grasp the medical dimensions of our struggle complements rather than opposes faith. God created us, knitting us together in our mothers' wombs, and our bodies are loved and cherished by Him. To minimize or generalize this element of our existence in favor of the spiritual is unbalanced and the opposite of incarnational faith.

But more than this, leaning into the medical side of infertility requires more, not less, faith. No doctor—no medical procedure or opinion or advancement or technology—can give you certainty, and your physician will be the first to admit this. The medical realm is simply an extension of the life we live everywhere else, a life whose mystery and uncertainty are made more meaningful when we "walk by faith and not by sight," even as we do not feel at home in our own bodies (2 Cor. 5:7).

It takes faith to walk into a fertility specialist's examining room for the first time. It takes faith to wake up every morning before dawn to test our basal body temperature for signs of ovulation, or to head out for diagnostic appointments. It takes faith to accept the limitations of our (or our partner's) body with love rather than despair. It takes faith to wait (and wait!) for the cause of all this to reveal itself. It takes faith to make sense of all the tests, results, answers, next steps, medical advice, and pastoral counsel. It takes faith to keep the door open but not set our hopes on these things. It takes faith to pray for the billionth time. It takes faith to act or not act, to move on or continue waiting. And it takes faith—a whole heck of a lot of it—to do all of the above, for months or even years on end, never knowing how or where this story will end.

This kind of faith is impossible to sustain alone, in isolation from others. It asks us to dig deep into the core of what it means to be a human or to follow Christ, and to do this we need the Church. But even bearing our struggle alongside other Christians—broken people just like us—requires still another dose of faith and vulnerability. In the following chapter, we will discuss both the challenges and opportunities that infertility presents us with in the Orthodox Church.

REFLECTION AND DISCUSSION QUESTIONS

1. How have your perceptions of infertility changed at different points in your life and why?

2. In this book, I tend to use *infertility* and *barrenness* interchangeably. Do these words mean the same thing to you? Why or why not?

3. In what ways is infertility bound up with mystery? How has infertility invited mystery into your own life?

4. In the section "Reimagining Sterility," I argue that no one is truly incapable of bearing life. Do you agree or disagree with that statement? Why?

5. What additional myths surrounding infertility would you add to the five that were discussed in this chapter? What do you wish more people knew about infertility?

CHAPTER 2

Infertility in the Orthodox Church

$\mathcal{N}$*ot long after I began* writing and speaking, I was invited to give a set of talks at a multi-day retreat put on by a lovely, medium-sized parish. During a coffee break on the first day, an older woman approached me. Within a few minutes of casual conversation, I learned she had grown up on a Greek island and had a scant dozen grandkids.

"Do *you* have children?" she asked me, a knowing glimmer in her eyes. I confessed I did not.

"Well, when are you going to slow down and have some babies? You are so busy!" she replied, knowing virtually nothing about my daily schedule, still less about the infertility my husband and I had just been diagnosed with. It felt like someone had ripped the carpet out from underneath me.

"We're doing our best. Pray for us," I replied, not because I am inordinately pious but because asking for prayer just happens to be both the nicest and swiftest way I know of to shut down intrusive remarks.

This time, though, the woman followed my request a bit too . . . literally. The next thing I knew, her hands were on my stomach, her eyes closed in what I can only assume was silent prayer. Other parishioners turned from their coffee conversations, baffled. *Is our speaker having appendicitis?* Their collective consciousness seemed to be asking itself of my pale face and abdominal activity. Then, all at once, embarrassed recognition swept over everyone's faces. *Oh.*

Before I could back away, a few other older ladies were on the scene, having flocked to my barren womb like seagulls to fresh fish.

"She's in her thirties and can't get pregnant," the first lady explained, as though filling a medical crew in on the condition of a gunshot victim arriving in the ER. They snapped into action, touching my hands and stomach, cooing and clucking in primordial sympathy. There was also talk of St. Irene.*

"Ladies, I don't know whether to hug you all or knock your heads together," is what I *wanted* to say. In reality, I just stood there. Mortified. Incredulous. A little touched (literally and figuratively).

It was among the strangest, most loving yet embarrassing moments of my life.

The next day, one of the women hauled a huge icon of St. Irene into the church. She presented it to me at the morning coffee break with such volume and gusto that half the parish turned to watch.

"St. Irene will help you," she explained. "Pray to her."

And I have.

The Greek old ladies who introduced me to St. Irene are a microcosm of the Church at large, a body that extends through time and space into the particularities of our lives. My encounter with them

---

* St. Irene the Wonderworker, a ninth-century abbess at the Monastery of Chrysovalantou in Greece, is a beloved saint particularly among Orthodox people of Greek origin. While associated with a wide array of miracles, her intercession is particularly sought out by couples who are unable to get pregnant. Eating apples blessed near the icon of St. Irene on her feast day, July 28, is one of several commemorative practices that the faithful have traditionally called upon for miracles of healing.

illustrates both the best and worst aspects of being childless in the Orthodox Church. This is a spiritual community that has much to communicate about the experience of infertility but doesn't always manage to speak with the best words, beliefs, or actions it is capable of. As a result, Orthodox contexts can serve as a source of both support and stress for childless couples. Alongside faith and religious beliefs, this is a milieu where non-Western and even premodern cultural mindsets still shape understandings of fertility and gender norms. This may at times be experienced by younger generations as offensive, intrusive, and hurtful (many more adjectives come to mind, but I'll stop there).

On the other hand, I maintain that interactions like the one above also illustrate the best of what the Orthodox Church imparts to the human condition. They show an empathy and honesty, if meddlesome, that is largely absent in mainstream attitudes toward infertility. In today's complex landscape of shifting social norms and family configurations, it is not so much infertility but the *grief* of infertility that is stigmatized. Because women can now "have it all"—in large part with or without men or stable relationships—infertility seems like a silly thing to lament. Just find a surrogate mother, or a sperm donor, or adopt—or throw yourself into your job, lifestyle blog, etc. And men? Men, so the stereotype goes, never really wanted the responsibility of children in the first place; they'll be fine.

However invasively, the encampment of ladies around my empty uterus reminded me of two aspects of infertility we tend to forget today. First, the inability to conceive is an undeniable tragedy. Life is a God-given gift, and when that gift is withheld or delayed, it should bother us—not just privately or individually or silently, but collectively, sometimes even in the middle of coffee hour, to the chagrin of over a hundred innocent and vaguely horrified bystanders. In their own bizarre way, these women get it. They know that no one should face that pain alone—just as it takes a village to raise a child, it takes a church to help someone face childlessness.

But they also taught me that as painful and frightening as infertility is, it's also just another part of life, not a taboo to be hidden or discussed in whispers. Part of what made their actions so jarring was that I am accustomed to people being afraid or put off by the whole topic. These women weren't. They weren't afraid to touch me and my pain; they weren't afraid to barge in on my private ash heap, set up camp there, and mourn alongside me—then force-feed me *kouloura-kia* cookies as though nothing had ever happened in the first place. Welcome to the Orthodox Church.

How is infertility grief experienced differently in Orthodox settings than elsewhere? While I welcome readers of other faith traditions, this chapter is specifically devoted to the unique factors that affect Orthodox couples struggling to have children. My aim throughout is to highlight not only what Orthodox couples can learn from the Church, but what we as the Church can learn from these couples— about being human, about parenthood and learning to love others, and about salvation.

"One of the hardest things was when our parents started asking when they could expect to have grandbabies. We finally sat them down and explained we needed them to be patient. We all cried together because it was something we all wanted but didn't have a complete picture of whether this was even a possibility." —Sophia

CULTURAL AND SOCIAL CHALLENGES FACED BY
ORTHODOX COUPLES WITH INFERTILITY

Orthodox couples with infertility encounter specific social and cultural challenges when navigating expectations surrounding childbearing and childlessness in the Church. These are intensified by the generational divides and non-Western cultural mentalities that typically characterize Orthodox parish life. While it may be comical to think of the stereotypical Greek (or Arab, or Serbian, or . . .) yia-yia foisting lamb and fertility advice on unsuspecting brides, variants of these interactions do occur in real life and are usually less endearing than their Hollywood portrayals. "I honestly dread going to coffee hour or other social events at my parish," Chrisanthi admitted in the *Under the Laurel Tree Questionnaire.* She explains why:

> It's a rare week when I'm not cornered by at least one other woman asking me for an update. Am I pregnant yet? For the millionth time, no. From there, the conversation shifts to advice. Have I tried the apple of St. Irene? Have I gone to this or that monastery? Tried this or that vigil oil? It's embarrassing and stressful. Meanwhile my husband just goes and talks to his guy friends, they don't give him grief about not having kids. I can never relax at church because I never know when I'll be blindsided by comments and questions.

What Chrisanthi describes is what I not-so-happily term the "infertility inquisition," a barrage of unsolicited questions and advice that leave one feeling vulnerable and defensive. And while the particularities she shares may seem extreme to some, especially those in less ethnically affiliated parishes, the general anxiety she describes is common to many Orthodox dealing with infertility. Most of the time, it is understood that a couple's intimate life and struggles are off limits in casual conversation. But once infertility enters the picture, it can somehow become socially acceptable for others to scrutinize even the most sensitive details of their relationship.

Reading between the lines, perhaps one of the most vexing elements here is not so much *what* is being said or asked, but *where* these interactions are taking place: at church. We tend to have higher expectations of people we encounter in parish life—they are Christians, they should know better. We also have higher expectations of ourselves, making it more difficult here than elsewhere to extricate ourselves from uncomfortable conversations or set appropriate boundaries. We don't want to risk appearing "disrespectful" or "rude," especially among other Christians. After all, didn't Christ bear His Cross unto death? (Yes, but He also called people out rather frequently before that.)

Another point Chrisanthi's experience illuminates is the tendency for infertility inquisitions to be aimed disproportionately at women. For whatever reasons, the kinds of comments and questions she mentions are more often voiced in female company. Thus, we ladies often feel we are on the frontlines of childlessness in a way our male partners simply aren't (or can't be). Not only does this diminish the sense of belonging and acceptance childless women feel when at church, it also leaves some husbands feeling inadequate.

I've heard from Orthodox men who are painfully aware their wives face more intrusive conversations about infertility than they do, but also feel unable to do anything about it. This can subtly compound the sense of powerlessness and emasculation they already feel in response to childlessness. "I sometimes overhear people talking to or about my wife like our infertility is her fault or something. They never ask about me or my part in this. It makes my blood boil," Victor wrote in response to the Questionnaire. Similarly, Mark described how inadequate he feels hearing about these kinds of interactions from his wife: "The worst part is, there's not much I can do about it. It would just make [my wife] feel worse if I randomly started confronting people on her behalf."

Still, childless husbands sometimes get their own portion of the social awkwardness. "What about that guy at the funeral last week?" my husband recently reminded me. A few days ago, he attended a church funeral for the father of an acquaintance. At the visitation, he got to talking with a friend of a friend, a grandfatherly gentleman he hadn't seen in several years. When this man learned we (still) didn't have kids, he immediately began offering "man-to-man advice" to help him "make it happen." My husband stood there patiently as, I'm told, angles were prescribed (not angels, my friends, *angles*). And pantomimed. Punchline: *At a funeral.* Needless to say, just when I think life with infertility (and Greeks) can't possibly get any more ridiculous, I'm proven wrong.

"*When my wife and I found out about our infertility, my mother asked me privately if we were going to separate. For her, an inability to conceive still constitutes legitimate grounds for divorce, despite being raised Orthodox.*" —Victor

To be fair, many of these more extreme examples involve people of older generations. Folks in this category seem equipped to speak about childbearing and its discontents with an authority and brazenness younger age groups aren't. This can be a great comfort when offered with love and respect. But when this expertise is proffered via confrontation and meddlesome advice (not to mention pantomimes), it can be disastrous. To complicate matters, many older people in our parishes hail from cultures in which it is perfectly normal for older people to "nudge" (read: force at gunpoint) younger generations towards procreation.

If any of this resonates, you are probably not going to win this battle—not if winning means trying to get an eighty-year-old matron to stop obsessing over expanding the ~~Greek~~ human race. Instead, find a way to laugh (you'll go crazy if you don't) and then (lovingly) set some boundaries. One way to do this is by tasking inquisitors with something to do. Calmly assure them you are doing everything in your power to, shall we say, improve the situation, and clearly explain that their questions are only stressing you out. "But here's what *would* be helpful," you can say. And then ask them to pray for you at home, light a candle for you, give your name to a monastery next time they visit, anything you can think of that is within their skill set. Giving them something to do helps them feel they are supporting you, which—strange as it may seem—is usually the intention behind inquisitions to begin with.

"*I found it difficult, as a woman, to see my friendships with other women shift as they became mothers. They were busier than I was. I struggled, and often failed, to fill my mind, heart, and schedule with pursuits other than the goal of having children. The things I was filling my life with seemed less interesting and important than my women friends who would talk a lot about their lives as mothers. The whole experience was isolating, at least on one level, and yet it was also very humbling and challenging and even inspiring, on another level. As I struggled to connect with my friends, I grew to really value the time I spent in prayer.*" —Teresa

OTHER SOCIAL CHALLENGES AT CHURCH

What about the less extreme difficulties childless people may face in social settings? I'm talking about the perennial, garden-variety challenges: trying to feel you measure up to the men and women in your social circle, being the only woman without children at yet another baby shower, what to complain about when everyone else is complaining about parental sleep deprivation. And as long as we're being honest, sometimes just showing up at church—unpregnant belly and all—and standing there in our own skin, week after week, year after year, broadcasting our childlessness for all to see, is the hardest struggle of all. Maybe it's the darling tow-headed toddler who crosses herself like an angel, maybe it's the screaming four-year-old in the row ahead of us whose action figures have been taken away until after Liturgy. Whatever it is, there's something about church that makes us feel even more barren than anywhere else on the face of the Earth.

"I still feel excluded in Orthodox women's groups as I do not have any offspring or grandchildren. I understand women with children have unique trials and joys, but it is definitely hard to maintain friendships when the major discussions are about being a mother or grandmother." —Lorna

I wish there were simple advice to ease the burden. The only wisdom I've found helpful is the adage "in all things, moderation." This applies to those who are infertile and those who wish to support them. For those of us who long for children, it is helpful to find a middle ground between disconnecting ourselves from social engagement and the bizarre yet real temptation to overcompensate for our situation by trying to be all things to all people at all times. Don't walk away from *every* tough or parent-centered conversation; after all, we are called to bear one another's burdens, and parenting issues are legitimate burdens many people face. By the same token, though, we don't have to throw ourselves into every such conversation just to prove we can handle it. Neither do we need to keep our infertility struggle *separate* from these conversations—we can find ways to bring it up organically, because this is a part of our life and experience.

And in a way, childlessness *is* a parenting issue. It's also something more people (and young parents) can relate to than one might think—many couples with children have faced miscarriages, for example, and can often relate to infertility through that lens. A similar perspective might be helpful for people who interact with childless couples. It's okay to bring up your kids or parenting and its challenges. But maybe not every single time, or at the expense of the other person getting to share their experiences.

I've been learning the value of this over the last year, since the mission parish we recently began attending is relatively small and composed of a variety of family configurations—singles, married couples with and without children, married converts attending without their spouses, divorced people, just to name a few. It is the only parish I've ever encountered where no single family type is in the majority—there are simply too few of us, with enough diversity that we are all coming from slightly different places. This forces us to discuss life challenges and struggles in ways that extend beyond the particularities of our personal circumstances. It also gives us permission to offer support to one another even though we may be coming from very different perspectives.

I don't know how long this dynamic will last as our parish grows, but for now it's helped me see my infertility in a new light. In the Church, everyone gets a place at the table—and in the ordinary conversations that occur *at* that table. I don't have to hide my predicament under a bushel because it isn't pleasant, or worry I will take time away from the more "normal" conversations about parenting stress. But neither do I have to rub it in people's faces or fight to be heard. It's a give and take, or rather a giving and receiving. In Christ, there is neither Jew nor Greek, male nor female, married nor unmarried, fertile nor infertile—which is to say there are all these things and more, but we shouldn't limit our dignity as human beings to these distinctions.

That said, there may be times when navigating social dynamics within your parish proves truly difficult (or even toxic) as a childless person. Some churches just "do" infertility better than others. If people's comments and questions make it difficult to feel at ease in church, and you've tried unsuccessfully to carve out a place for yourself, it's worth bringing to the attention of the priest. He may genuinely be unaware of what it is like to be a childless person in his parish and need some suggestions to steer conversations in a healthier direction (Appendix I of this book is a great place to start!). Plus, it's unlikely you are the only one suffering—the same attitudes that negatively affect childless couples in a parish also tend to affect single people or others who, for whatever reason, don't fit the nuclear family mold.

❧

"There are many in the Orthodox world who have a number of children and express this almost as a status symbol. In a recent visit with our bishop, he said he was going to make a rule that everyone in the diocese needed to have

twelve children. He was joking, but it was only he and I in the
car and he knows my situation. It was very troubling to see
the pastoral blindness with such a comment." —*Aaron*

INFERTILITY AND PASTORAL CARE:
CHALLENGES AND OPPORTUNITIES

Infertility represents a complex and often overlooked area of pastoral counseling. While I am thankful that the priests who pastor me approach this issue with understanding and wisdom, this is not always (or even often) the case in the Church at large. Responses to the *Under the Laurel Tree Questionnaire* revealed many experiences of priests or bishops chastising couples with infertility by making light of their childlessness ("Are you just too tired at night to try?"), criticizing couples with fewer offspring than the ideal, or otherwise dismissing the pain and spiritual questions infertility raises. The ministers in these situations seemed mostly oblivious not only to the hurt and mistrust their comments caused, but also to the fundamental possibility that a couple may be childless for reasons beyond their desire or control.

Pastoral ignorance on this issue perhaps stems from the statistical reality that most clergy haven't experienced infertility firsthand and so cannot grasp the complex grief and marital stress it can create. But according to Fr. Geoffrey Ready, mentioned in the introduction of this book, it may also be due to the fact that "the Orthodox spiritual tradition is naturally oriented towards ideals of *beauty* and *wholeness*, inherited from both Greek philosophical aesthetics and the Hebrew concept of the glory of creation." He acknowledges that while most of the time, this emphasis is more helpful than juridical or transactional models of salvation, there are situations when "it falls short in helping us understand and deal with aspects of disability and human experience."

Having personally faced miscarriage, infant loss, and periods of infertility with his wife, Fr. Geoffrey observes:

> Families struggling with infertility are by default viewed as "not normal," and despite theological protestations that sickness does not result directly from personal sin, they are too easily suspected of some kind of secret sin. I can remember being asked by a sincere parishioner when our infant daughter died what God was trying to tell us about what was wrong in our lives! This shunting of the not-beautiful and not-whole to the margins is often expressed liturgically as well, as for example in the service of marriage which is replete with prayers for children and grandchildren—prayers which must prove difficult for those who already know that they can't have children to hear, or who will look back on these prayers later in the midst of infertility. Good pastoral ministry always starts with listening, and we need to hear the voices and stories of those who don't "measure up" to our pre-conceived ideals of beauty and wholeness, and maybe in hearing those stories we will come to understand that none of us quite measures up to those ideals anyway.[13]

Fr. Philip Rogers, an Orthodox priest who recently adopted a baby girl with his wife after trying for over ten years to have a biological child, reiterates this idea. "Pastoral ministry to the infertile," he says, "is largely one of loving presence. It is a time to weep with people and allow their struggle to be heard. There is nothing comforting to say nor are there any good platitudes, it is simply one of weeping together. This is how all grief should be handled, but with other situations, there are often some words that are appropriate. In this case, there really is not."[14]

Some may take issue with this statement. Isn't *some* advice or guidance warranted? At the very least, shouldn't couples be warned of the Church's position(s) on assisted reproduction? What we tend to forget is that infertility-related advice touches on some of the most intimate, mysterious, and fragile areas of a couple's union. Moreover, even the most innocuous and spiritual-sounding suggestions—particularly when unsolicited—can inadvertently send the message that infertility is the fault of the couple. When offered by a priest or other clergy member, this advice—and the latent sense of shame and failure that comes with it—only carries more potential for damage. According to Fr. Geoffrey:

> We are quick in the church to take an issue such as infertility and make it an abstract question of ethics or theological reflection, but what people need most of all is acceptance, love, and accompaniment through their suffering and grief. What I try to convey, not only to students preparing for pastoral ministry but to all people I minister to, is that every family and every home conceals a considerable amount of trauma, suffering, and grief—we have no idea what people have had to endure in their lives. We must therefore approach every human being we meet with as much compassion as we can. Infertility, miscarriage and infant loss are all part of that hidden pain that a great people carry with them and rarely share.[15]

Speaking from personal experience, it seems there is a time for all things—a time to grieve with our priest and others, a time to be still, and a time to ask for advice or talk about next steps. But underneath all these different "times" is the continuous need for attentive listening, acceptance, and robust compassion. Early in my infertility, I appreciated that the priests in my life did little more than remain calm and available. They were quick to listen and pray, slow to express judgment and opinions. Because of this, I learned to trust them with my grief, anger, and resentment towards God. That I am able to write this book is in large part testimony to the fact that they not only allowed me to do so, but helped me integrate my grief with faith in a God who is supposedly life-giving.

Eventually, when my husband and I did have questions and wanted to begin thinking about next steps, we knew we could let them into our decision-making. We are still "in process," so to speak, but we trust the priests we have consulted to offer answers and resources in a spirit of co-suffering humility rather than authority or judgment. Also helpful is that our priests seem consistently less concerned with *where* we end up in our infertility (whether we will get pregnant, adopt, etc.), and more interested in *how* we will end up there. Will my husband and I make decisions as a united team? Will we be intentional rather than impulsive? Will we consider our options with prayer and trust rather than fear and shame?

Still, as helpful as my own priests have been since we encountered infertility, I wish the conversation on this issue had started long before we encountered problems conceiving. I've talked to many Orthodox couples across North America—few if any recall infertility being brought up during premarital counseling sessions. Children, and the stress that raising them entails, were the unquestioned expectation. I believe, however, devoting time to infertility during premarital counseling serves three important purposes. First, it counterbalances the assumption that children come automatically, reminding us all that life is God's gift and every marriage is unique. Second, it helps prepare couples for the possibility of infertility and the sources of tension that can arise from it. Third, for couples who will never end up facing this issue personally, these premarital conversations raise awareness of infertility and help minimize its stigma in parishes.

One person who took the *Under the Laurel Tree Questionnaire* suggested that infertility be brought up even earlier, in youth and young adult groups, alongside conversations on relationships, sexuality, and theological anthropology. While we can't (and perhaps shouldn't seek to) erase the pain of infertility, having these conversations early and often normalizes what can otherwise be a shame-inducing and often-misunderstood blight on a marriage.

There are many other practical ways we can learn to stand alongside and help bear the grief of infertility in our parishes—I've gathered what I've learned from others in Appendix I of this book.

INFERTILITY AS A FORM OF ASCETICISM

The Orthodox faith has a rich tradition of asceticism, the idea that a person can attain a more unhindered relationship with God through rigorous self-denial and spiritual labor. On a daily basis, we remember the many men and women over the course of history who voluntarily died to the world and adopted a life of prayer, poverty, and intentional solitude. For us, their stories are more than ossified historical artifacts; they continue to be a part of our living tradition and inspiration in a way that may baffle outsiders.

"I struggle with feeling guilty about not grieving our childlessness enough. I know in my mind and heart of hearts that I would like to have children, but at the emotional level I do not feel utterly desolate at the thought of being childless forever, and I haven't cried about my infertility. This gives space for a voice to whisper that I'm a failure as a woman: surely if I really cared about motherhood I'd be sobbing myself to sleep every night. I know that this voice is a lie, and that God has formed our individual temperaments in different ways. But visits to infertility clinics and most literature on infertility (both secular and often religious) make it more

difficult to silence this voice, since they present an image of
pregnancy as an ultimate good to be achieved at any cost."
—Brianna

Infertility involves more self-denial than many people realize. In an age where luxury and achievement are so often the measure of success, it can pose a real conflict to our values and ideals. Asceticism provides a corrective, reframing our struggle and sense of failure, and allows us to see this journey as a kind of purposeful desert. This is not to trivialize the lives of "real" ascetics but to remind us that the deaths infertility brings into our lives do not signal that something is "wrong" with us in a spiritual or salvific sense. The ascetical core of our Tradition affirms that suffering, when we adopt it with a willing and voluntary spirit, can enrich rather than impoverish our experience of life.

How does infertility embody a form of asceticism? For one thing, it narrows certain aspects of our everyday lives—it is its own kind of fasting season. And I mean that literally, not just metaphorically. Many ordinary daily choices—from coffee and wine intake to the foods you eat to your stress level and exercise habits—now become scrutinized, filtered through their propensity to negatively affect one's fertility. Fasting from animal products during Great Lent is one thing; cutting back on a caffeine addiction while trying to conceive is . . . quite another matter.

Then there are the many tests and doctor appointments that require logistical juggling and balancing. And we haven't even mentioned the whole world of timing (and timing!) and waiting—and then repeating the whole cycle next month. Even sexual intimacy can become a cross when subjected to that kind of stricture. Finally, there's praying, and praying, and more praying. However you look at it, to stay in the game of trying to conceive, even just a little bit, means a lot of little deaths-to-self. Obviously, this is not the same regimen monastics undertake (not sure a diet of locusts and honey, not to mention sexual abstinence, is fertility friendly) but their fortitude and self-surrender give us an icon of how to welcome meaningful struggle into our lives.

And the biggest death, the biggest point of self-denial, is surrendering ourselves to the possibility that even despite all our efforts, children may never come. Just as Abraham and Sarah and so many others lived faithfully without ever beholding the face of Christ, the ultimate promise of their salvation, so we may never live to see children. Sometimes when I voice this realization aloud, others gasp a little and caution me not to give up. For them, surrendering seems almost antithetical to faith or hope; they are afraid if I give into it too much, I'll stop doing what I need to do to get pregnant. But they haven't ever struggled with infertility, certainly not as long as I have. They haven't had to live for years on end with hopes stretched thin like a rubber band between possibility and pain, always waiting for it to snap back in your face.

Here's what I've learned: surrender is not resignation or acceptance (more on this in Chapter 7). It's not about giving up for the future, but being more fully alive in the present, operating outside the confines of constant fear and franticness. I can draw from a deeper place when I'm operating out of surrender. They say that the sensation of pain—physical or otherwise—is exacerbated by resisting whatever is hurting you. If my back hurts and I spend the whole day obsessing about it, wishing the pain weren't there, it will literally feel more painful. Likewise, if I spend my days fixating on infertility, trying to change it, or worrying about what the rest of my life will be like without a child, the pain grows exponentially. But if I just let it be—not ignoring my pain but acknowledging and surrendering it to

Christ—the sharp edge of worry diffuses. The reality is, I *am* childless right now, and look: the world is still standing. I'm still alive. It feels so feeble sometimes, but there is much to give thanks for if I turn my gaze from my worst anxieties to what is all around me. To me, this is the essence of hope rather than its opposite.

It feels like the beginning of prayer. I simply can't pray with my whole heart when I'm so caught up in fear and resentment that I've grown hard and unyielding. And prayer, we already know, is the whole point of asceticism. It's not about vain self-mortification or setting Guinness world records with one's fasting abilities. It's about narrowing and deepening one's focus so that the soul becomes more capable of bearing and reaching out to Christ. Infertility, if we let it, will begin to do this. It will shrink the whole world of life down into this microcosm of suffering, and allow us to taste at least some of the fruits of the prayer and total dependence on God that those souls who hid themselves "in the deserts, on mountains, in caverns, and in the chambers of the earth" were so familiar with.[16] In this, childlessness becomes our teacher, our elder in the wilderness. We may not always leave with the teaching we came for, but if we listen and attend, we are sure to find the wisdom we most need.

"*Extremely fertile Orthodox people can be insensitive in their statements about the number of children faithful Orthodox should have, etc., even when you have shared some of your infertility troubles with them (at great personal expense, emotionally)."* —Randi

NO PREGNANCY IN HEAVEN:
INFERTILITY AND THEOLOGICAL ANTHROPOLOGY

What does it mean to be human? How do we understand our nature as creatures in relation to God? These are the guiding questions of Christian anthropology. Although this avenue of theology has its origins in apostolic-era and patristic writings, it is today among the most vital fields of inquiry in the Church, given the impact of rapid social and technological changes on our understanding of the human person. Yet the question of what it means to be human tends to be approached from a handful of conventional, almost predetermined paths and texts. Articulating a robust theological anthropology for a postmodern, twenty-first-century milieu will undoubtedly require venturing outside the box of our standard repertoire, in part by mining previously overlooked sources of knowledge about human experience.

I believe infertility represents one such repository, a crucial and as-yet unexamined facet of what it means to be human. Infertility—under the premodern nomenclature of barrenness and childless-ness—features as a predictable, if perplexing, leitmotif throughout the Old Testament. Each time God moves to reaffirm or expand His covenant with the people of Israel, a prominent couple finds them-selves unable to conceive. By the end of Genesis, this pattern is so predictable you can almost set your clock (biological or otherwise) by it. In the end, the couple always bears a child, but only after intense prayer and crying out to God. In patristic and older Jewish inter-pretations, this was generally viewed as a sign concerning the person to be born, an indication of the special role he would play in God's covenant with His people. But I often wonder if barrenness isn't also an indication of something bigger, deeper, and more fearful—an icon of humanity's true nature as creatures whose very being is contingent on God's love.

In other words, what if barrenness is not a pathological but normative aspect of human existence?[17] What if it is not infertility but fertility—the capacity to participate *at all* in the life-giving process—that is unnatural, unexpected? These questions provide a starting point for reflecting on the salvific meaning of barrenness and its import for theological anthropology.

The earth, upon its inception, was formless and void (Gen. 1:2). Regardless of the English rendering of these words, in the original Hebrew and in the Greek Septuagint they were tied to emptiness and chaos. It seems the natural state of things is barrenness, or even nonexistence. God the Creator brings forth life. It is He who, as is so poignantly described in the Book of Job, "stretches [the North] over the empty space" and "hangs the earth upon nothing" (26:7, NKJV). And it is He who, in accordance with His self-emptying love, fills the barren womb of creation's non-existence with life.

Moreover, from the earliest decades of Christian thought, it has been largely assumed that there will be no childbearing (or sexual intercourse) in the Eschaton. While some ancient cultures and religions may have envisioned the afterlife as some kind of procreative playground, in the Judeo-Christian imagination, it is in many ways a return to (or resanctification of?) barrenness, which is to say a return to the self-emptying and everything-filling love of God, of which human reproduction is merely a shadow.

This is not to minimize or spiritualize the travail of infertile couples, but rather to validate the almost cosmic dimensions of their grief, which has been numbered among the most difficult traumas a person can face. (And the very fact we grieve infertility tells us we are more than the material sum of chemicals and evolutionary biology— we yearn for new life, to participate in its inception, to bear it within us.) What is it we are actually grieving? Psychology tells us it is the loss of certain roles, identities, hopes, and dreams for the future. But, deep down, from the vantage point of our God-given human-ness, I wonder if we are not also grieving the prospect of our non-being. We are grieving the fact that our existence—and that of all creation—is not merely beyond our control, it's not even necessary. Barrenness, even the mere possibility of it, brings us to the brink of dissolution. It leads us by the hand back to a primordial precipice, where we see in stark relief the normal state of things when viewed apart from God, and reminds us that none of this had to be. The sole reason we exist, and can hope that anything at all will continue to exist, is by virtue of being known and loved by an eternal, self-giving God.

As an intellectual, it is easy for me to "know" these theological principles concerning creation and humanity's place within it. But, as a childless woman, to *feel* barrenness in my body is entirely other. More than anything else in my life, it has caused me to face the full, awe-ful magnitude of humanity's dependence on God. I don't know why God gives infertility to some couples and not others. But I do know that they who find themselves in this place will—knowingly or unknowingly—bear witness (the literal meaning of what it means to be martyred) to an element of our humanity that perhaps cannot be communicated to the world in any other way.

"Infertility has strengthened my prayer life, but also the understanding that God does not answer all our prayers positively." —Dorothy

CONCLUSION

On first glance, the Orthodox Church may pose certain social and emotional challenges for childless couples. At the same time, the active presence of these same couples in parishes poses a meaningful challenge for the Church. Ultimately, I believe both sets of challenges can be fruitful ones. In the case of the Church, infertility gives us first of all an opportunity for repentance. How have we missed the mark when it comes to encouraging and supporting those dealing with infertility grief? I can recall instances where I, too, have manifested less than the full measure of love toward my childless brothers and sisters.

Second, acknowledging and ministering to the needs of childless couples helps guard against one-sided and even judgmental assumptions about human conception, family life, and God's will. In learning to listen to the grief infertile couples express, we learn to move past the nosy questions and subtle ostracism, past the stereotypes and taboos—all of which usually mask our inability to embrace uncertainty—and stand with them on the shores of barrenness and the God-filled mystery of creation. In doing so, we gain crucial insight into the human condition and the roots of our salvation.

Childless parishioners, too, can find meaningful opportunities for growth in the Church, even when surrounded by imperfect and at times unloving people (aren't we all?). Infertility is like a school for our souls. It presents us with continuous interpersonal opportunities to strengthen our weak limbs and build joy instead of jealousy, hope instead of hopelessness, thanksgiving instead of cynicism, prayer instead of feebleness. And as many times as we have felt judged or neglected, we have the chance to learn (and relearn) that most basic manner of being for the Christian: forgiveness.

But we are also given the opportunity to learn how to speak the truth in love. Forgiving and loving does not mean you neglect all sense of personal boundaries and self-worth. It's okay once in a while to say *no*, or *that hurt*, or *that's kind of you but no thanks*. It's also okay, sometimes, to say yes—*yes, I will take that icon; yes, I will receive that vigil oil; yes, I will find comfort in your words*. This, too, is something we can glean from the difficult interactions our childlessness so often seems to precipitate: that we are both worthy and capable of guarding our well-being and the well-being of others.

Whether we are childless or child-ful, male or female, clergy or laity, may we strive to be and become loving members of the body of Christ in the presence of infertility, as elsewhere.

REFLECTION AND DISCUSSION QUESTIONS

1. What are the social and cultural difficulties you or others face in the Church with regard to infertility?

2. Have you ever faced an "infertility inquisition"? If so, how have you handled it?

3. How has the Orthodox Church either enriched or challenged your experience of infertility?

4. In what ways did this chapter's presentation of infertility challenge your views or understanding of fertility and barrenness?

5. What can the Church learn from couples who struggle with infertility?

CHAPTER 3

Joachim and Anna in the Protoevangelium of James

Against all hope, the bonds of barrenness are loosed today. For God has hearkened unto Joachim and Anna clearly promising that they would bear a godly maiden. He who commanded the angel to cry out to her, "Hail, full of grace, the Lord is with you," will be born of her, the infinite One Himself, becoming man.

—APOLYTIKION OF THE CONCEPTION
OF THE THEOTOKOS (DECEMBER 9)[18]

Do you have those saints who feel like friends? Saints who seem to show up, mystically, to guide you, to be with you, to pray for you? Saints who, despite the expanse of time, space, and human mortality, feel *present* in your life in a way that others are not?

I don't—at least not in the way others seem to describe. One might assume that writing an entire book on Saints Joachim and Anna probably means I've had some kind of earth-shattering, life-changing encounter with them; that we three are, in the epic deadpan of Napoleon Dynamite, "pretty much friends by now, right?" But you'd be wrong. I've never been visited by either of them (that I know of), nor have I experienced an evident miracle through their intercessions. What draws me to them is neither goosebumps nor warm fuzzies, but their story—their shame, struggle, prayers, and thanksgiving.

Truth be told, the only thing I knew about these saints before becoming Orthodox was that Martin Luther, ten years before inaugurating the Reformation, vowed to St. Anna he would become a monk if she preserved his life during an unusually terrifying lightning storm. Ever the Protestant at the time, I assumed she was some minor medieval saint whose veneration Luther would later repudiate, so I never bothered to look her up. Even years into my Orthodox journey, I barely noticed the curious line at the end of the Divine Liturgy that commemorates "the holy and righteous ancestors of God, Joachim and Anna." Who were *they*? I'd ask myself on the rare occasions I managed to think about anything by that point in the Liturgy besides the coffee and food waiting in the fellowship hall. Eventually, of course, I realized they were the parents of Mary, thus making them the grandparents of Christ, but for a long time even that remained little more than an isolated fact—something that might prove helpful in a trivia game.

It was only after getting married, particularly once our infertility manifested itself, that I began to crave stories of married saints— people who managed to work out their salvation in and through the royal martyrdom of matrimony. And the story that brought me the most comfort was that of Joachim and Anna. As N. T. Wright says, "Tell someone to do something, and you change their life—for a day; tell someone a story and you change their life."[19] The story of Joachim and Anna has certainly changed my life, and in that, I suppose they *have* become—if not intimate friends—then certainly beloved mentors. If you haven't met them yet, allow me to make an introduction . . .

*"Tell someone to do something, and you change their life—
for a day; tell someone a story and you change their life."*
—N. T. Wright

REMEMBERING SAINTS JOACHIM AND ANNA

Although never mentioned in Scripture, Joachim and Anna have long been revered in both the Christian East and West (and, incidentally, in Islam) as the parents of Mary. Their story was first expressed in writing in the *Protoevangelium of James*, the second-century text upon which this book is based and which narrates the birth and childhood of the Theotokos as well as the Nativity of Christ (see Outline of the *Protoevangelium* below). In the centuries since they lived, the trappings of Joachim and Anna's story have been preserved and embroidered upon in hymns, icons, hagiography, and festal commemorations, all of which have contributed to a multilayered memory of these beloved saints.

That rich story has been consolidated, among other places, in *The Prologue of Ohrid*, a popular nineteenth-century compilation of Orthodox hagiographies and prayers originally written in Serbian:

> St. Joachim was the son of Varpafir from the lineage of Judah and a descendant of King David. Anna was the daughter of Matthan the priest from the lineage of Levi as was Aaron the high priest. . . . Anna married Joachim in Nazareth and, in their old age, gave birth to Mary, the Most Holy Birth-giver of God. Joachim and Anna lived together in marriage for fifty years and were barren. They lived devoutly and quietly and, of all their income, they spent one third on themselves, the second, they distributed to the poor and the third, they offered to the Temple. They were considerably well-off. Once,

when they, in their old age, came to Jerusalem to offer a sacrifice to God, the high priest Issachar reprimanded Joachim saying: "You are not worthy that a gift be accepted from your hands for you are childless." Others, who had children also, pushed Joachim back as being unworthy. This greatly grieved these two aged souls and, in great sorrow, they returned to their home. Then the two of them gave themselves in prayer to God, that He work a miracle on them as He once did to Abraham and Sarah and to give them a child as a comfort in their old age. God sent His angel, who announced to them the birth of "a daughter most-blessed, by whom all nations on earth will be blessed and through whom the salvation of the world will come." Anna immediately conceived and, in nine months, gave birth to the Holy Virgin Mary. St. Joachim lived for eighty years and Anna for seventy-nine years and then presented themselves to the Lord.[20]

The above passage summarizes the important plot points in Joachim and Anna's life as recalled by the Church—the joining of Anna's priestly and Joachim's kingly ancestry; their long years of barrenness; their shame in the temple; and, of course, the miraculous conception and birth of the Theotokos.

As will become clear in later chapters of this book, this brief account differs slightly from the more literary and dramatic depiction of Joachim and Anna found in the first chapters of the *Protoevangelium of James*. Not only are some of the above details absent from the *Protoevangelium*—like the precise lineages of Joachim and Anna, and how long they had been married before conceiving (fifty years)—but in some cases the two accounts conflict. For example, in the Protoevangelium, it is not the high priest who ridicules Joachim but a figure of unknown rank named Rubim. That account also depicts Joachim in the temple by himself, without Anna, and instead of returning home to her after being rejected there, he flees to the desert, causing Anna to grieve him as though dead.

Tradition is messy and often multi-stranded. To me, this has always testified to the humanness of Holy Tradition, a humbling reminder of the risk God takes in allowing His children to tell His story. If the devil is in the details, I think that God is most often found in the bigger picture—steering and guiding and whispering this storm-tossed ship of a Church toward what is good, beautiful, and holy.

These discrepancies remind us, first, that tradition is messy and often multi-stranded. As a Church, we remember saints through a variety of accounts, not all of which align perfectly. To me, this has always testified to the humanness of Holy Tradition, a humbling reminder of the risk God takes in allowing His children to tell His story. If we waited for human memory to be healed of its frailty and cognitive disconnects before venerating saints, we would likely have forgotten about Joachim and Anna a long time ago. Regardless of who exactly reprimanded Joachim in the temple, or whether Anna stood beside him when it happened, or any other granular facet of their story, it is the humble, faith-filled act of veneration—not our modern preoccupation with historical inerrancy at all costs—that has not only preserved the memory of these saints but animated it. If the devil is in the details, I think that God is most often found in the bigger picture—steering and guiding and whispering this storm-tossed ship of a Church toward what is good, beautiful, and holy.

The second reason I have pointed out some of these discrepancies is to introduce us to the *Protoevangelium of James*, the oldest text where Joachim and Anna's story is found. Taking a closer look at this book, and the problems it can sometimes present, gives us a more careful and nuanced understanding of the plight of Joachim and Anna as it will unfold in subsequent chapters of this book.

OUTLINE OF *THE PROTOEVANGELIUM OF JAMES*

Under the Laurel Tree is based only on the first five chapters of the *Protoevangelium*, which convey Joachim and Anna's childlessness. This is only a small portion of the *Protoevangelium*, which also narrates the early life of Mary up through the birth of Christ.

» Chapters 1–5a: The barrenness of Joachim and Anna

» Chapter 5b: The birth of Mary

» Chapters 6–7: Mary's infancy

» Chapters 7–8: Joachim and Anna bring Mary (age 3) to live at the temple

» Chapter 9: Mary (age 12) is betrothed to Joseph

» Chapters 10–21: Annunciation of Mary and the birth of Christ

» Chapters 22–24: Zechariah and Elizabeth preserve the life of John after Herod's decree against the innocents

PROBLEMS WITH THE *PROTOEVANGELIUM*

If I were to describe the reception of the *Protoevangelium of James* among Orthodox Christians using a Facebook relationship status, I'd say "it's complicated." On the one hand, the *Protoevangelium* provided the narrative content for several prominent Marian feast days, particularly the Conception (December 9), Nativity (September 8), and Entrance of the Theotokos (November 21).[21] In its account of Christ's Nativity, the book also testifies to the ever-virginity of Mary, an important teaching of the Orthodox Church. Even today, it is not uncommon for Orthodox priests to incorporate elements from this book into sermons and other catechetical instruction.

Yet the *Protoevangelium* wasn't always regarded favorably. As an apocryphal book, although it features key individuals and events of the Gospel narrative, the *Protoevangelium* was never a serious contender for the New Testament Canon. First, it most assuredly was not written by James (neither the kinsman of Christ nor any other James associated with Him), despite the author's own claim to the contrary in the closing lines of the book. (The mid- to late-second century, when the book was most likely written, places its inception some three generations after James was martyred.) Early Church Fathers, if they knew about the text at all, seem to have been reluctant to grant it much credence, likely because its depiction of biblical events departed somewhat from that of the Gospels.[22] For example, in the *Protoevangelium*, Herod slays the innocents at the time of Christ's birth, not two years later (as in the Gospels).

According to Mary B. Cunningham, the *Protoevangelium*'s authority remained an "open question" in the Christian East until the sixth century, when some liturgical writers began drawing on it in their hymns and homilies. The reason for this shift, as she sees it, was the institution from the sixth century onward of new feast days—such as the Nativity, Annunciation, and Dormition of Mary—that centered on the life of Mary and her status as Birth-giver to God. "Since the Gospels do not provide the full story with regard to Mary, apocryphal sources . . . were used to fill the gap." The *Protoevangelium* provided both narrative and theological inspiration for such liturgical writers as St. Andrew of Crete and St. John of Damascus. By the eighth century, at the latest, it seems that the *Protoevangelium* had "achieved full acceptance in the Byzantine liturgical and theological tradition."[23]

In contemporary circles of Orthodoxy, some regard the *Protoevangelium* with suspicion and reticence. While I believe discernment and critical inquiry should be applied while reading any book, perhaps some of the current contention surrounding this book in particular stems from its categorization as a "Protoevangelium," or infancy Gospel, a popular second-century literary genre that focused on Christ's birth and early childhood. In actuality, however, only a limited portion of the *Protoevangelium* is devoted to the birth of Christ, and even that section focuses less on Christ and more on the saintly figures surrounding Him: Mary, Joseph, Elizabeth, Zechariah.

Reading this book in its entirety, it soon becomes clear that this is less a "Gospel" than a hagiography—and a somewhat legendary one at that. In the Church, there are many hagiographies that are not historically literal or verifiable down to every last detail. We read them in part because we believe that, in telling these stories, we are invited into something more "true" and edifying than a history textbook could afford. Apocryphal or not, the *Protoevangelium* has long captured the imagination of the Church and, alongside other vehicles of Holy Tradition, has helped lift our gaze to the wonder and struggle that brought Christ into the world.

Infertility disrupts the narrative arc we always assumed our lives would follow. What will we do with our lives? How will we fill our time meaningfully? What comes next? These questions—though perennial to the human condition— crescendo the longer one walks through the valley of the shadow of barrenness.

ENCOUNTERING JOACHIM AND ANNA
IN THE *PROTOEVANGELIUM*

There are many biblical and extrabiblical texts and stories on which one could base a spiritual book about infertility. I chose to write about Joachim and Anna—in particular as their story is captured in the *Protoevangelium*—not because it is the most authentic or historically reliable source, nor because of the way it has shaped veneration of the Theotokos, but primarily because of its healing influence on *me*.

Philosopher Richard Kearney put it beautifully when he wrote that "human existence is a life in search of a narrative."[24] In few circumstances is this truer than in the grief of childlessness. Infertility disrupts the narrative arc we always assumed our lives would follow. It's a loss that extends beyond the present into the distant past, accompanied by the nagging sense that one has been betrayed by childhood dreams or has somehow disappointed one's forebears. It also extends into the distant future; after all, an empty womb signals not merely the absence of a child *now*, but the loss of that child's potential future and progeny—the loss of an entire legacy. What will we do with our lives? How will we fill our time meaningfully? What comes next? These questions—though perennial to the human condition—crescendo the longer one walks through the valley of the shadow of barrenness.

The first time I read the story of Joachim and Anna as an infertile woman, it comforted me—if I'm honest, in a way no account of barrenness ever had, even those in the Bible. The sadness and raw struggle of these two saints—and their subsequent gratitude—breathed hope into the weary parts of me that, for once, didn't depend on whether I'd ever get pregnant. But that initial comfort was only the beginning. Rereading (and rereading!) and remembering their story over time has transformed my perception of my own grief, allowing me to frame my otherwise senseless experiences within theirs.

Thus when I receive a (usually unintentionally) unkind comment about my lack of children, the memory of Joachim in the temple reminds me others have borne this unique shame with courage. When my husband and I are at an impasse, or I have isolated myself in my sadness, I remember that even Joachim's time in the desert was temporary. When intrusive and unsolicited advice makes me want to pull my hair out in frustration, I recognize it as a "headband from your handmaiden" moment (a reference that will make more sense in Chapter 6) and I try to remember—with Anna—not to forfeit my soul. And in seasons of furious and frantic prayer, I can see myself not lost or unmoored in my grief, but beneath the laurel tree, with God, perhaps moments away from the healing balm of thanksgiving.

One way scholars refer to this transformative quality of story is as *enacted narrative*. When we step into stories of salvation and take them on as though they were our own, they have "the potential to restore and reform us because [they] *re-narrate* our identity, drawing us into the narrative arc that replays and re-enacts the story of God reconciling the world to himself in Christ."[25] The reason the story of Joachim and Anna is healing and life-giving is not simply that the author of the *Protoevangelium* knew how to tell a good story, but that at its core, it is a story that points to Christ—how He came to be in the world, despite (and because of) great loss and barrenness. For me, leaning into that—activating both the grief and the thanksgiving I have learned from Joachim and Anna—has helped me begin to tell a new story, not only about my childlessness but about the love of God for us.

As we turn to the chapters that follow, it is my hope that their story helps transform your own grief as well.

REFLECTION AND DISCUSSION QUESTIONS

1. Do you have saints who feel like friends? How have the lives of saints enriched your journey through infertility or other losses?

2. What story has brought you the most comfort in your grief journey? It could be a biblical story, or a literary one, a movie, or even a personal experience. What is the most edifying or encouraging element of this story?

3. What are some of the "problems" with the *Protoevangelium?* Do you agree or disagree with the assessment presented in the chapter?

4. Consider the quote by Richard Kearney mentioned at the end of this chapter: "human existence is a life in search of a narrative." What part of your story has been most disrupted by infertility? In what ways has this fueled a search for a new narrative?

5. As we turn now to the story of Joachim and Anna in the next section, what do you hope to find? What is one area of your grief you could particularly entrust to their intercession?

PART II

The Five Stages of Joachim and Anna's Infertility Grief

CHAPTER 4

The Shame of Comparison

*In the records of the twelve tribes of Israel was Joachim, a
man rich exceedingly; and he brought his offerings double,
saying: There shall be of my superabundance to all the people,
and there shall be the offering for my forgiveness to the Lord
for a propitiation for me. For the great day of the Lord was at
hand, and the sons of Israel were bringing their offerings. And
there stood over against him Rubim, saying: It is not meet for
you first to bring your offerings, because you have not made
seed in Israel. And Joachim was exceedingly grieved, and
went away to the registers of the twelve tribes of the people,
saying: I shall see the registers of the twelve tribes of Israel,
as to whether I alone have not made seed in Israel. And he
searched, and found that all the righteous had raised up seed
in Israel. And he called to mind the patriarch Abraham, that
in the last day God gave him a son Isaac.*

—PROTOEVANGELIUM OF JAMES, I

"A MAN RICH EXCEEDINGLY": WHERE TO BEGIN?

There are many ways one *could* begin a story about a couple and their childlessness. There's the "cold open" of Genesis 16, when—with no warning—we are thrown into the plight of Sarah (then Sarai): "Now Sarai Abram's wife bare him no children" (16:1, KJV). Then there's the "where do we even begin" segue into Jacob and Rachel's fertility struggles: "When the Lord saw that Leah was hated, he opened her womb: but Rachel was barren" (Gen. 29:31, KJV). Clearly childlessness was the least of the issues going on here. Recall that Jacob had only married Leah as part of a bargain to obtain her sister, Rachel. Fertility seems to have been God's consolation prize for Leah, who was never Jacob's first choice, but this only incites rivalry between the sisters.

By the time Leah is on her sixth child, Rachel has gotten pretty desperate. "Give me children, or else I die," she raged at her husband (Gen. 30:1, KJV). Not only did her impatience seem to have been a turnoff for Jacob (whose anger, we are told, "was aroused against Rachel" after her plea, 30:2), but it doesn't seem to hasten things in the pregnancy department. Two concubines, some extorted mandrakes, and oodles of dubiously conceived stepchildren will pass before Rachel finally conceives a child of her own: Joseph. *Whew.*

But these and other Old Testament depictions of infertility have one thing in common: they almost invariably start with women— their inability, their shame, their desperation. This makes the story of Joachim and Anna all the more distinctive. Instead of a desperate woman, there's a rich and self-assured man. Instead of a closed womb, there is an absence of "seed." This uncharacteristic focus is often the first thing people notice when they read the *Protoevangelium* for the first time. Even by today's standards, when male experiences of infertility remain under-researched and overlooked, this alone makes Joachim and Anna's story revolutionary.

The point is this: How we frame stories is important. It signals what to pay attention to, whom to watch, and how to settle ourselves into the narrative that's about to unfold. And enveloping the arc of infertility within the experience of Joachim rather than Anna disrupts expectations we may not have even realized we had. Of course, this is just *one* text—and a rather literary (as opposed to historical or scriptural) one at that. Still, when viewed through the eyes of faith, it's perhaps a foreshadowing, the first of countless ways Christ's swiftly approaching entrance into this world would reverse the normal order of things. We are introduced to shame through the alternative entryway into childlessness: the male perspective.

And what does childlessness look like from this vantage point? By the end of this vignette, it appears that despite his having spent his entire life in service of God, the doors of righteousness were as closed to Joachim as Anna's womb was to his seed. As he contemplated his grim future, Joachim found himself turning backward, through the layers of the salvific past, toward the memory of Abraham, who in God's graciousness had been granted a son "in the last day." Inasmuch as Joachim drew strength from Abraham's story, we are invited to do the same, to turn our gaze from our present predicament and find comfort in someone who has already traveled this path in faith: Joachim himself.

This chapter reflects on Joachim's experience as a point of entry into the shame of infertility, particularly as it relates to social ties both within the couple and without. By mapping the phenomenon of shame and the different ways it affects men and women in the context of infertility, we learn how to start recovering connection and empathy.

"Shame plays a big role in communication, or lack thereof. I have tried to keep some of my pain private, as I know it will cause my husband to feel powerless to fix the thing that hurts me most. In that way, we each suffer alone." —Emilia

WAKING UP TO SHAME

Many of us who have struggled to have children are familiar with the kind of shame Joachim experiences. Perhaps we, like him, can even pinpoint that moment we recognized that we were "different" from other couples around us—bad news in a doctor's office, another negative pregnancy test, another pregnant friend. For Joachim, that spark of awareness happened in the temple. One moment, for all Joachim knew, he was a faithful and favored man of God with nothing to be ashamed of; the next, it was as though his entire self-worth before God and man alike had been a lie. But as rude an awakening as this was, it was a long time—or rather an eternity—in the making.

In his letter to the Galatians, St. Paul proclaimed that God sent His Son into the world "in the fullness of time" (Gal. 4:4). Some translations render this phrase as the "right" or "appropriate" time. It's a temporal convention that has to do with *kairos*, the time of opportunity, of critical action, of eternity bisecting chronology. In art, kairos is sometimes personified as a young man with a bow and arrow, capturing the swift precision with which kairos moments cut through ordinary historical time (*chronos*). If we believe in a God of divine intention, a God who weaves all things together for good, it follows that the Incarnation didn't just occur at any random moment. It happened at the best time, the time that was most advantageous for God and man to draw closer to one another (even if the specific criteria for such a time may remain inscrutable from our earthly vantage point). I like to remember this when I read and reflect on the lives of Joachim and Anna. They, too, were bound up in this timing. What was it about them and their place in history that made them fitting, opportune grandparents for the Son of the Living God?

According to tradition, Joachim and Anna had been married for fifty years prior to conceiving the Theotokos—that's a half-century of barrenness. You'd think that after so many decades, they'd be rather forlorn about their predicament—or at least *aware* of it. But when their story begins, Joachim doesn't seem concerned about his lack of children. He looked to virtue and meaningful activity for a sense of purpose, becoming "a man distinguished in holiness and righteousness" and "notable in nobility and wealth," to borrow the words of seventh-century lay preacher Kosmas Vestitor.[26] Indeed, so "single-minded in his offerings of sacrifices"[27] was Joachim that, until this point in his life, he seems virtually oblivious to the fact that his wife remained barren, or at least that this should be a source of embarrassment and castigation.

It is only when Rubim calls out Joachim's childlessness that shame enters the picture. We watch as he suddenly awakens to the reality that he is different (in a bad way) from other men of Israel. By prohibiting Joachim from bringing his offerings *first* in the temple, Rubim uses Joachim's lack of progeny against him and undercuts what shame researcher Brené Brown would call Joachim's "worthiness," what we in the Church might call his "dignity," and what others might more candidly call his "manhood." However you refer to "it," Rubim's insult was a low blow. All at once, Joachim becomes "consumed with desire for a child," in his panic checking the registers for any indication that he is not absolutely alone in this condition.[28] No luck.

The truth settles in. The ugly cloud of shame unfurls, cloaking for a time the light of God's favor from Joachim's sight. It is the first frame of what will be a long journey of grief.

❧

"I guess I have experienced this grief differently than my wife in that I have a feeling of being out of place, not knowing where to go from here, since the life that I had always pictured didn't seem to be coming together." —Gregory

❧

WHAT IS SHAME?

For only five letters, shame is a big word. It is, in many ways, elemental to the human condition. But what is it? Brené Brown defines shame as "the intensely painful feeling or experience of believing that we are flawed and therefore unworthy of love and belonging—something we've experienced, done, or failed to do makes us unworthy of connection."[29] Three points stick out to me in this definition. First, shame is personal and interior—it's a response or belief within and about ourselves that may not be evident to others. Second, however inward shame is, it has drastic effects on how we relate to others outside ourselves. It drives us to disconnect and distance ourselves from relationship out of a deeply rooted sense of unworthiness or inadequacy.

❧

"We talk about women's bodies as life-giving, so when your body is not able to give life, and in fact feels like a tomb, it can be detrimental to one's self-worth. My sense of failure

*carried over into all areas of my life, making me feel like I
was completely unsuccessful at everything."* —Eva

Finally, shame is a value judgment, not a neutral or objective belief—in other words, it is not a fact but an opinion. In shame, we notice something about ourselves (our empty bellies, our weight, what we've done or not done over the course of our lives) and assign a negative value to it. Others could see the same trait but assign a completely different meaning to it. For instance, when I enter a room full of women who all have children, I immediately see my childlessness in a negative light. I believe this thing that differentiates me from them makes me bad and less worthy to be part of that group.

Yet if were actually to say that out loud (not that I EVER have, because I am NEVER AWKWARD), the other women would respond with surprise and incredulity—it likely would never have occurred to them that I was the only one without kids in the room, much less that I would fear their judgment. "Honestly, sometimes I wonder why you want to hang out with *me*. I always feel like I don't measure up to you," a mama friend once confided after I spilled the beans about my secret shame. It turns out the whole time I'd been feeling inadequate around her for my lack of mothering experience, she'd been feeling dumb for her lack of a graduate degree. It just goes to show: at the end of the day, these shameful comparisons we build up for ourselves are usually deceptive.

Shame is commonly contrasted with guilt. Many of us have heard the saying that guilt is about something you've *done*, while shame is about who you *are* (or at least perceive yourself to be). But here's another important distinction: guilt can be adaptive and productive; it signals when your behavior does not match your values so you can make transformative changes. Shame, on the other hand, is often unproductive and destructive because there's nothing you can do or alter to alleviate it. You can't change who you *are* any more than you can change the eye color you were born with.

This whole doing/being, productive/destructive contrast especially resonates when we think about infertility. The shame that builds up around this condition cuts particularly deeply. It goes beyond a sense of regret or loss over an incapacity to *do* something (i.e. bear children) and encompasses who we *are*. It is the pain of *being* (or feeling ourselves to be) lifeless, barren, empty, impotent, and unworthy.

"I battled bouts of depression solely around our inability to get pregnant. And I began to let terrible thoughts creep in, such as 'Maybe we weren't getting pregnant because God never intended us to be a married couple.' I know I wounded my husband greatly by expressing these fears, and we are still working to improve our relationship so we never get to that point again." —Sophia

"IT IS NOT MEET FOR YOU": COMPARISON AND JOACHIM'S SHAME

Just as in Joachim's case, shame almost always begins with a comparison, or rather a contrast. Whether prompted by our own observations or the ridicule of others, shame is a reaction to the sense that at our core, we are somehow different from "the pack," the social fabric of belonging. The sense of comparison can also be fueled by contrasting our ideals with reality.

In infertility, we may perceive ourselves to be different from or even inferior to:

» "normal" couples;

» the way we are "supposed" to be;

» the way we thought/wanted our lives and marriage to work out;

» that lucky sister-in-law, who seems to get pregnant about as often as she shares a water bottle with her husband;

» our parents, who married young and were already done having children by the time they were the same age we are now.

As I mentioned before, shame is not the neutral valuation of difference but a subjective judgment. It involves recognizing differences like those above and assigning an automatically negative meaning to them. It's saying "Infertility has made my life and marriage different than I expected, and this is bad/wrong/an embarrassment."

Although these shame-based judgments can be incredibly painful, they are usually a product of our own imagination. What I mean is, no one is actually *telling* us we aren't a normal couple or our childless marriage is worthless. If they are, they are most assuredly crippled by far more shame than we are—hurt people hurt people, as the saying goes.

Rubim may well have been one of these "hurt people." There is no obvious evidence, in the Law or elsewhere, that Joachim would have been forbidden to bring his offering simply on account of his childlessness. According to Timothy J. Horner:

> Not being able to produce a child was often seen as an act of God, but whether this ever meant that childlessness could disqualify one from offering gifts at the temple is unknown. But this may be nothing more than Reubel [alternate spelling of Rubim] taking the law into his own hands and publicly shaming Joachim. Reubel is not

necessarily a priest and may have simply been jealous of Joachim's wealth and prosperity. . . . Regardless of Reubel's status or motives, Joachim feels publicly shamed and retreats into isolation. [30]

Far from a true exegesis of the Law, Rubim's taunts were a thinly veiled power play, an attempt to knock the "exceedingly rich" Joachim down a few notches. In my neck of the woods, we call this a classic jerk move.

Which raises the question: Why would Joachim—a righteous and evidently level-headed guy—pay so much attention to such a petty person? After all, Joachim doesn't just get a *little* upset about this interaction; he falls apart at the seams. It throws his whole self-concept into a tailspin, and he eventually risks his marriage and his very life to resolve it. Clearly Rubim had struck a nerve. Perhaps we can explain Joachim's intense reaction in sociological terms—men, so the cliché goes, experience relationships through hierarchy. When their place in the pecking order is threatened, it can be devastating.

But I believe Joachim's sudden-onset humiliation runs deeper. If you read between the lines of some currents of ancient Judaism, the shame of childlessness fell more heavily on men than on women. While biblical accounts of barrenness typically center on women, at least one Jewish tradition held that men could also be held culpable for lack of progeny in marriage. The context of this surprising acknowledgment is found in the Mishnah (Yevamot 6.8), where several rabbis are debating the circumstances in which it is lawful for a husband to abstain from intimate relations with his wife when the marriage fails to produce offspring. They conclude that "One may not abstain from procreation unless he [already] has children." In other words, guys: if you haven't had kids yet, get back in the bedroom.

The rabbis carefully note that even after ten years, a man is not allowed to abstain from intimacy with his wife. The end of this debate is fascinating and surprising: "A man is commanded to procreate but a woman is not. . . . It states to both of them, 'And God blessed them and He said to them . . . be fruitful and multiply.'"[31] While the meaning of these final sentences is difficult to pin down (was God telling both of them or just men to be fruitful?), the implication of the text is that in some traditions of Judaism, men could be held just as responsible for childlessness as women could. Horner interprets Joachim's response to be driven by this ethos—even as Rubim's specific pronouncement seems to have been unfounded, it played on broader cultural and religious attitudes towards childless marriages that were likely at work in their milieu. It is thus conceivable (no pun intended) that Joachim felt not only ashamed of Anna's barrenness but also gravely responsible for it—and not merely before Rubim or the other men at the temple or even Anna, but before God Himself, to whom he had given his entire life in service.

"There have been some priests and bishops who have literally asked, 'What is taking you so long? Don't you want children?' Or even suggesting that it is a necessary expectation, that procreation is how we populate and ensure the future of the Church. It is our service to the Church. What is a polite response? 'By your prayers.'" —Emilia

"HE CALLED TO MIND ABRAHAM": CONNECTION, THE OPPOSITE OF SHAME

Once when I was struggling with shame, I asked a friend what she does to defeat it. A two-time survivor of cancer and the unabashed recipient of a double mastectomy, she is one of the most confident, resilient people I know. "The opposite of shame is calling a friend," she told me. Shame, she reasoned, makes you feel unworthy of human connection. As a result, we pull away from loved ones, coworkers, church groups, or even public spaces and crowds. My friend's point was that we can only begin to think and act outside our shame by seeking connection with others. I've remembered her words; on many occasions, making contact with someone or something outside myself does help counter the darkness of inadequacy.

The reason this works is that shame makes us feel "trapped, powerless, and isolated."[32] Shame is a response to something we *are*, how we perceive ourselves at the core of our being, and is difficult to fix or hide from. But seeking connection with others allows us to give and receive empathy, the ultimate destroyer of shame. Connection is such a powerful antidote to shame that it is one of the four pillars of Shame Resilience Theory, a recently developed area of knowledge concerned with how people respond to and heal from feelings of shame. A 2006 study by Brené Brown found that our shame resilience increases even if the connection we forge involves supporting others rather than receiving support ourselves.[33]

Still, calling a friend is often easier said than done, especially if shame has already trampled us down. In the above-mentioned study, Brown speaks of the "reaching out continuum," which is "the measure of one's ability to reach out to others to both find empathy and offer empathy" at any given time.[34] In the depths infertility brings into my own life, I can occasionally feel myself stepping backwards on this continuum—avoiding people or interactions I would ordinarily welcome, finding excuses to become more solitary or reclusive. I know other women who have gotten rid of social media accounts or stopped going to church as frequently because the pain of seeing everyone's children grow up was too great. In the long run, however, avoidance like this can often increase rather than decrease shame.

We may not always possess the vulnerability required to actually call a friend and tell them of our struggles, shame, or feelings of powerlessness. But sometimes it's enough to pet a dog, feed a fish, or spontaneously help an old lady reach something from the top shelf at the grocery store. Sometimes simply *remembering* those we love, or our ancestors, or our friends is enough to bring us back into connection.

In a certain sense, this is precisely what Joachim did by "calling to mind Abraham." Just as we call on saints for comfort and intercession, just as we might call a friend in our despair, so Joachim recalled Abraham. In doing so, he flipped the script—Rubim's words *weren't* the final truth. There *was* another man in Israel who hadn't produced seed, and he became the father of God's people.

∞

"What others tend to not understand about infertility grief is the loneliness. No matter how strong my relationships are with others, or how much I pray, I am almost haunted by a profound sense of alone-ness in this world." —Liz

∞

EXPERIENCING SHAME AS MEN AND WOMEN

Joachim's shame response ties into some crucial differences in how men and women process this emotion. Recognizing and valuing these differences is a vital part of tending to infertility grief well as individuals, couples, and communities. In casual conversations, I often hear other women say that their husbands "just don't understand" or "aren't as upset as they should be" about their lack of kids. They're not the only people who believe this. If popular portrayals of infertility in movies and media, and to some extent even scholarly research, are any indication, men are still in caveman mode when it comes to the pain of childlessness and paternal responsibilities in general. But these kinds of depictions are dangerous because they plant the seeds of confirmation bias, which grows until anything our husbands do is interpreted as apathy or self-focus.

My personal theory is that, if men *do* appear to be emotionally withdrawn from this conversation, it's at least in large part because of shame. It's not that women don't also struggle with infertility shame, but the rules of relational engagement are such that we have more freedom to express it in constructive ways. Even when infertility is not on the table, for all sorts of reasons, men tend to have fewer socially acceptable tools for expressing their shame in relationship rather than in isolation (which, as we've discussed, is not a great way to alleviate shame). Showing vulnerability and need is not easy in a culture that vilifies men one minute and expects them to be unassailable fortresses the next. When you factor in infertility, which is experienced by many men as a threat to masculinity (more on that in a bit), there are even fewer options to express vulnerability without damaging their reputation as males even further. Adding this all up, it's no wonder some husbands may initially seem more closed off or insensitive when it comes to childlessness than their female counterparts—they *do* have feelings, but if they indulge them, it may open up a flood that will have no place to go.

For now, let's give ourselves a break and assume that whether we are male or female, our partner is struggling with just as much infertility shame and pain as we are. When we adopt this starting point, we remain open to possibility and a better understanding of our spouse. In doing so, we often find that the shame of infertility revolves around different things for women and men—and that's okay, even beautiful.

"*People marry for different reasons and for some, a main reason is to procreate. When you can't give your spouse what they wanted in a marriage that is a strain on you. You question whether the other person will still want you as a partner or if the marriage will be strong enough to survive as it leaves a hole for both people.*" —Angela

"*My sister has many children. She says I don't make it very easy for her to tell me when she's pregnant. She feels like she's hurting me and that she doesn't have a right to be happy, which makes me feel like an evil woman.*" —Bethany

Infertility shame in women

To distill countless conversations I've had with other women in this predicament, it seems that for women, infertility shame stems from a powerful sensation of physical emptiness or lifelessness. We feel that something is unnatural about us physically or anatomically. The womb lies at the very center of a woman's body, and our sense of barrenness, emptiness, or just plain *wrong*-ness is just as deeply rooted within us. With time, this physical sense of emptiness may expand to affect our whole self-concept. Instead of seeing ourselves as women who happen to be in possession of barren wombs, we may begin to see ourselves as barren, full stop—cold, harsh, inhospitable, un-nurturing, insufficient, a waste of space. Emptiness becomes a way of being in the world, a defining characteristic, something we imagine others notice about us a mile away.

The physical contours of women's infertility are intensified by the fact that, in a couple's struggle to conceive, women's bodies become a sort of battleground. Even if a husband and wife decide against invasive treatment, the woman's monthly cycle serves as a physical, recurring reminder of their childlessness. When trying to get pregnant, it is difficult to experience the arrival of your cycle as anything other than a harbinger of your failure or incapacity as a woman. And that does not even begin to touch on the intrusive tests used simply to diagnose infertility in women, which are necessarily more intense and even painful than they are for men (by virtue of our entire reproductive system being located *inside our bodies*). Women never have the luxury of running away from their barrenness or its implications for very long—even in the most remote desert, our menses or continuously empty womb are always with us, always reminding us.

Because of this, women may come to feel betrayed by their bodies. We may go in and out of seasons where we feel disconnected from them, as though they were dirty or uncooperative. There is some indication that infertile women, particularly those undergoing fertility treatment or assisted reproductive procedures, are more likely to experience a loss of libido. If that's true, it seems likely to me that the reason has far less to do with the loss of our sex drive as such or our attraction to our partner, and more to do with our lost sense of trust in ourselves. We are haunted by the possibility that our infertility isn't accidental or superficial, that it has somehow revealed our bodies to be what we feared all along: undesirable, damaged goods, unlovable.

Yes, it's true that our shame as infertile women is triggered by other more superficial situations as well—being the only childless guest at a friend's baby shower, the only cousin at the family reunion who hasn't gotten pregnant yet. But for many women, these more external grievances are simply symptoms of that deeper shame I described above, the voice that tells us something much darker and more elemental is wrong with us than the fact we don't (or can't) have children.

❦

"Even years later, infertility still impacts my sense of womanhood to some degree with every new person I meet. There is always the question of 'how many children/ grandchildren do you have?' Not 'do you have . . .' but 'how many?' It is still a stab in my heart." —Lorna

❦

"I wish more people realized that men can want children too; we are not solely interested in pursuing a career. Also, it is sexist and incorrect to assume that infertility is primarily a problem with female biology; men can be infertile too."
—Zach

❦

Infertility shame in men

While infertile women may experience shame in connection with *physical or bodily* inadequacy, for men shame more often stems from feelings of *sexual* inadequacy. Almost across the board, men equate infertility with some degree of emasculation and loss of virility. As a post-sexual revolution society, we collectively roll our eyes when we hear this kind of thing, citing the supposed neediness and fragility of the male ego. But when you think about it, sex is perhaps the only tangible thing men have to contribute to childbearing. They don't have a womb, they don't have menses to track, ovulation to time, symptoms to gauge. So when conception isn't happening, the first thing a man blames is, well, his manhood.

The scholarly literature on this subject is replete with examples of the ways infertility negatively affects men's sexual self-concept. Among other things, sexual dysfunction is more common among male partners in couples dealing with infertility than it is in the general population, particularly when a male factor like low sperm count has been determined. While this may be due in part to the psychological and physical stress of timed intercourse, it also stems from the shame men experience in response to infertility. Sexual dysfunction is a vicious cycle because it begets more embarrassment, thus compounding an already pervasive sense of lost masculinity.

Speaking as a woman, perhaps the most eye-opening part about my own infertility journey (I mean, aside from having my uterus inflated with saline during my first sonohysterogram, which was eye-opening in a wholly different way) has been coming to terms with how deep the shame of male infertility grief can run. In some sense, it's easier to believe men are emotionally distant or clueless than the alternative: that they feel in the very center of their being they are a failure, that they are more concerned for their wives' well-being than their own, that they would willingly die or disappear if it meant alleviating our distress.

"I feel, on some level, totally inadequate. It's not mental. It's not chemical. It's a depression in my very core," is how one man, quoted in a study on infertility grief, described the powerlessness he felt at being unable to provide a child for his wife. Another was even more blunt: "I wanted my wife to leave me, find a man she can love AND father her child. It was like, 'What's the point of marriage?' I literally wanted to just disappear."[35]

"*Husbands experience the grief of miscarriage and childlessness too, although in a different way that's easy to overlook. In difficult times like that, I think most husbands' first instinct is (correctly) to support their wives, to be there for them to lean on. While that is good and necessary, it can lead to men not sharing their own internal lives and how they are doing. I think it would be good for people to know that even if the husband doesn't say he's having a hard time and doesn't ask for help, he probably is having a hard time and needs other people he can talk to, including other fathers. I know from talking to other men that it can often manifest itself as random anger, too, although this was not my experience.*"
—Gregory

Infertility and social status

As my husband and I read this section of the *Protoevangelium* together, he pointed out something I missed. If I really wanted to understand Joachim's shame and why his response may continue to resonate with men even two millennia later, I have to acknowledge something that probably sounds politically incorrect today: children tend to be a form of social currency for men. Like a good wife and a purposeful career, having kids helps solidify a man's sense of place in the hierarchy of other men. Although today many couples voluntarily forgo having children (often termed "childfree" rather than "childless" partnerships), men who are *unable* to have children may find that their involuntary lack of kids destabilizes their sense of belonging among male peers.

Children, for women, help solidify horizontal connection. They provide entry into relationship with other mothers and can open up a new dimension in women's ties with their own mothers or other female relatives. For men, though, children are often about vertical connection. "They tell us where we are in the pecking order and help us keep our spot," my husband explained to me.

"That does not seem like a friendly world," I observed. I was reminded of studies I've read in which men with wives and children are often granted more professional opportunities than those without, presumably because they are deemed more responsible or capable.

"It's not that men don't have horizontal connections, it's just that we need to know where we are in the vertical scheme of things before we can really trust in those peer-to-peer friendships," he said. "I can't explain it."

But I think he explained it pretty well.

"My wife has never been one to fantasize about being a mother. I, on the other hand, have long wanted to be a father, even when I thought I would never get married. So it is quite an adjustment to consider a future without children. Sometimes I feel like I have to deal with infertility alone, without my wife's support, as she doesn't really understand what I am going through or feel that I am having a reasonable response." —Zach

Bearing vs. giving

I am struck by the divergent vocabularies I've often heard men and women use to convey their shame. Women tend to note their inability to *bear* a child, while men more typically associate shame with an inability to *give* to their wives—not just a child, but also emotional comfort in the midst of infertility. What a heartbreaking but beautiful contrast. It illuminates, I think, two complementary facets of being human as men and women. And it's a difference we should pay attention to in our marriages. It is not uncommon for women to complain or lament that their husbands aren't as sad about the absence of children as they are. From their vantage point, husbands may seem more upset that *their wives* are sad than by an actual lack of children, which can be feel a bit like abandonment. But is this a lesser pain, or just a different one? For the sake of our marriages, and our hearts, it's helpful to think in terms of the latter. Anyone who has ever observed someone they love in the midst of suffering knows how excruciating it can be to wish you could trade places or erase their pain. Some men I have met, at least on their hardest days, would just as soon die or go away if it meant their wives getting pregnant.

At the risk of sounding too reductive, perhaps a man's sadness at being unable to give life reflects the desire built into humanity to love self-sacrificially, specifically in the manner of the self-*giving*, self-emptying Christ. We can assume that the biological drive for procreation is as hardwired into a male psyche as it is for a female, yet in infertility grief (as elsewhere), men tend to operate outside of this basic impulse. Instead of grieving the lack of progeny and posterity, they tend to become more concerned about the emotional impact of barrenness on their wives. While they may also be upset about childlessness in itself, men tend to grieve their inability to *give* and *provide* enough of themselves to create life or to ease someone else's pain.

On the other hand, a woman's sadness at being unable to *bear* a child images humanity's God-given capacity and desire to be recipients of and participants in the incarnate love of God, that is to bear Christ—new Life—within our very selves, even as the Theotokos bore the Christ child in her womb. We often look at Old Testament renderings of infertility and bemoan the fact that childlessness is so frequently depicted as the woman's fault. Yet out of this human ignorance comes a hidden prophetic blessing—an icon of humanity's condition without or prior to Christ: barren. Disconnected from future Life. The Incarnation of Christ necessarily involved both bearing and giving—Mary's willingness to bear, God's willingness to self-give and pour Himself into temporal human existence through His Son. As intertwined as these impulses were, however, they could not be offered by the same being or at the same time. They required a call and a response, two entities—God and humankind—coming together, two faces encountering one another across the abyss of shame and separation, and choosing to draw even closer out of mutual love and freedom.

Infertility tends to bring the emotional differences between men and women to the fore. It's tempting to assume that these differences mean something is wrong with our marriage or our spouse. I recently heard someone say "You can be right, or you can be married." Similarly, I think that you can insist on a right way to grieve—or right *things* to grieve—or you can be married. We can resent and lament our differences, or we can embrace and embody the valuable, even salvific, meaning to be found in them, and from our respective corners of shame choose to step closer to one another. We each reflect an important piece of the same icon.

∞

"I think that my grief is that my body feels broken—that I cannot do the thing that (as a woman) I was born to be able

to do. I think my husband's grief is that he cannot fulfill my emotional need, or fix the thing that keeps me up at night or causes me to weep. I think that he feels helpless, and that as a man he is somehow failing as a provider for our family."
—Emilia

"IN THE LAST DAY"

I hate the physical sensation of shame. For me, the first wave of it almost knocks me off my feet with adrenaline—sweaty palms, racing pulse, a blushing face, the feeling that someone has just pulled the carpet out from underneath me. I almost always have an impulse to run away, to find something safe and private to hide behind so no one can witness the pathetic spectacle of who I actually am. Experts have nicknamed this the fight-or-flight response. Whatever it is, it's a reaction that must be as old as humanity itself. In the Judeo-Christian creation narrative, after their Fall, Adam and Eve hid from God and constructed clothing of fig leaves to cover their nakedness from Him.

Where did Joachim go in his shame? As we will see in the next chapter, he *did* go somewhere, physically, perhaps driven by a fight-or-flight impulse of his own. But first he retreats into a story, one that even in his day was as well-worn and familiar as a beloved friend: the story of Abraham. Like Joachim, Abraham had lived a life of God-centered purpose. Also like Joachim, he entered old age without a true heir (although Abraham had sired children through other wives and legal concubines, Sarah had remained barren). Finally, "in the last day," under a night sky aflame with stars, God promised Abraham that not only would Sarah conceive, but his descendants would outnumber the dazzling heavenly lights above. Of course we

UNDER THE LAUREL TREE

all know the ending to that story: God ultimately made good on His covenant, a promise to which Joachim owed his very existence as a child of Israel.

But what I find most interesting is that Joachim's first refuge from his shame is in a story. He doesn't counter Rubim's taunts with axiomatic belief or a well-reasoned exegesis of the Law. Even as he fails to see himself in the righteous, child-raising men of Israel, he maps his turmoil onto that of Abraham. In the midst of shame, we don't need to be reminded of isolated truths and doctrines, however relevant they may seem. We need to know, most of all, that we aren't alone. Somehow we are still connected to something—to our spouse, to God, to our peers, to this great illimitable journey of being human. We need to know we are somehow *like* rather than unlike other people—that the cause of our shame makes us closer to rather than more distant from those around us. And we need to know that as deep as the shame feels when we've lost the thread of our own self-narrative, the journey hasn't ended yet.

This, I think, is why we need to have stories, especially redemptive ones. We need to tell stories, and we need to listen to them. When someone expresses shame, we don't hand them advice or bioethical dilemmas or some trite syllogism ("Jesus still loves you"). We tell them "I've been there, I get it. Let me tell you about that time I walked out on stage with toilet paper stuck to the back of my skirt." And just like that, we've invited them back into connection.

And it's also why it's okay to lose (or rather, find) ourselves in someone else's story once in a while, to borrow another narrative for a bit, try on their mistakes and fears, brokenness and salvation. This is not a form of escapism; stories allow us eventually to return to our circumstances with more creativity and hope.

In Christian circles, we often speak of memorizing prayers or scripture verses so we may call on them in times of trial. I even know of handbooks that have specific verses under specific kinds of distress, for easy reference. But in a deeper sense, maybe we also need to have stories ready to tell ourselves in specific situations. The greatest of all stories, of course, is the Advent of Christ and all it brought about for our salvation. But really, all good stories are a movement toward salvation. If we can locate ourselves in the narrative of someone who, despite very real struggles, chose hope instead of despair, reconciliation instead of hatred, connection instead of disintegration, self-giving instead of self-loathing, we are already on the way to Christ.

Joachim and Anna's story has always been that kind of story for me, one that draws me out of shame and back into communion. And perhaps one reason for that is this detail, this moment where Joachim remembers Abraham. It tells me that he knew not only the scourge of shame but also the impulse to reach out to the saints and their stories for help. And even as I look to his story for comfort, I'm sucked as through a vortex into connection not just with him, not just with Anna, but with Abraham and the whole network of salvific lives that anticipated the coming of our salvation. Just as Christ came in the fullness of time, so too did Abraham receive Isaac in the nick of time, or "in the last day" as it says in the *Protoevangelium*. We know, of course, it was not the literal last day of all time, just the end of Abraham's waiting. And yet, in many ways, it was just the beginning.

And I suppose the answer to any despair, including our own, always comes at the most opportune time. When our shame feels more real than our hope, when comparison and ridicule seem more immediate than the love of God, when the emptiness of barrenness seems more persuasive than the fullness of grace, let us hold fast to the story—it's not over yet.

DISCUSSION AND REFLECTION QUESTIONS

1. What moment in this "frame" of Joachim's story did you most identify with and why?

2. What kinds of comparisons stoke the fires of infertility shame for you?

3. What could "calling a friend" and seeking connection mean for you?

4. In what ways do you think your husband's or wife's experience of infertility grief is different from your own? What would help you feel understood by your spouse?

5. What do you appreciate about your spouse's response to infertility? What have you learned from him or her?

6. What point in this chapter made the biggest impact on your view of infertility?

CHAPTER 5

Separation

And Joachim was exceedingly grieved, and did not come into the presence of his wife; but he retired to the desert, and there pitched his tent, and fasted forty days and forty nights, saying in himself: I will not go down either for food or for drink until the Lord my God shall look upon me, and prayer shall be my food and drink.

And his wife Anna mourned in two mournings, and lamented in two lamentations, saying: I shall bewail my widowhood; I shall bewail my childlessness. And the great day of the Lord was at hand.

—PROTOEVANGELIUM OF JAMES, 1–2

*W*hen we last left Joachim, he was still in the temple, seeking solace in the memory of his ancestor, the great patriarch Abraham, who "in the last day" had been given Isaac. Now the scene shifts; the reel of the great story of faith unwinds one frame further. Instead of returning home after his time in the temple, Joachim ventures into the desert. At first glance, his reasons appear pious; he is embarking upon a forty-day fast, perhaps inspired by the example of Moses or Elijah. But Anna experiences his retreat as a tremendous loss, one that heaps a whole new layer of mourning onto her childlessness. Not only is her womb empty, but now also her marriage.

What we encounter in this frame of the story is, in the truest sense of the word, a separation. A fissure. A marriage at a crossroads. The turn of events should surprise us—after all, Joachim and Anna seemed like a couple who had it all together, spiritually speaking. But perhaps this is the point. Even for the best of us, infertility grief can spark withdrawal from community, including marriage, fraught as it is with reminders of children and inward shame. As the geographic and emotional distance between these two holy figures widens, we remember how fragile shared life can be, even when it has been woven together in the fear and service of God. Ironically and perhaps prophetically, however, this will be the last scene of the *Protoevangelium* that features both Anna and Joachim until they reconcile. Their separation—and the healing of that separation—is the only part of the grief journey they truly share.

What does marital breakdown—and togetherness—actually look like in the context of infertility grief? This chapter reflects on the theme of separation from a variety of vantage points in order to examine where separation begins and how it ends. In the case of Joachim and Anna, if we know the story of our salvation, we are already aware that their withdrawal from one another is only temporary—they will eventually recover and reunite. But let's resist the temptation to fast forward to the happy ending. Instead, let's allow ourselves to dwell in this frame right along with them, not knowing what God will bring out of their sadness and fragmentation. In doing so, we remember that no marriage (no matter how holy) is immune to the seeds of dissolution, yet neither is any marriage (no matter how dysfunctional) fully outside the bounds of God's saving provision.

"*We've lost four children at this point and each time, I feel an irrational sense of failure. I feel that, as their father, it is my job to look out for them and keep them safe and that if they've died, it must be because I didn't do something that I was supposed to, or else that, since God is merciful, they must be better off without having me as a father to guide and raise them. That feeling is irrational, which I know in my head, but not always in my heart. It's also very personal and I've only really shared it with my wife and my confessor.*" —Gregory

ADAM, EVE, AND THE ORIGINS OF SEPARATION

In Orthodox readings of the first few chapters of Genesis, Adam and Eve's sin resulted in a tragic fragmentation that permeated all levels of creation. Like a crack spreading across the wall of an old house, this fissure separated not only man from God, but also man from woman, humanity from creation, and, finally, man from himself, from his will to be united with God.

In physics, the second law of thermodynamics holds that entropy (or disorder) within a single system can never decrease over time. In other words, objects and processes naturally move from order to chaos rather than the other way around—it is, and will always be, easier for an egg's shell to break open and spill its contents everywhere than for that same egg to somehow suck itself up and gather itself back into its pristine shell. The Fall of Adam and Eve wrote a similar kind of law into the fabric of creation, the law of fragmentation: people and circumstances more easily gravitate toward separation and dissolution than toward unity. The story of Adam and

Eve testifies to the power of one event to shatter wholeness, and the countless permutations of this brokenness continue to reverberate through our present lives.

⋙

"*Don't allow the evil one to use infertility as a tool to drive you from your spouse. It is arguably the most difficult thing you will face. You can get through this, but only with both sets of eyes turned toward God. Try to use this as a time to grow as a team and find a new purpose as a family unit. Resist the temptation to interpret infertility as a sign that your marriage is a failure.*" —Sophia

⋙

Infertility gives couples a rare glimpse of the magnitude of this brokenness. Technical and medicalized understandings aside, what is infertility other than an echo of the fragmentation that has afflicted fallen existence almost since the beginning? On the most primitive level, the inability to conceive involves the failure of two or more elements to come (or stay) together—man to woman, egg to sperm, embryo to uterine lining (don't worry, I'll stop there!).

And the ripple effects of this mode of separation extend beyond biology. In the Old Testament, for example, childlessness often seemed to evoke the worst in people and their relationships. I'm not talking about concubines and polygamy and other historical-cultural curiosities—I'm talking about the competition, the stalled conversations, the desperation, the lies. For all God's prophetic intention behind these narratives, I can't shake the nagging sense that somehow, barrenness has brought men and women to the very brink of dissolution as a twofold unit instituted by God in the beginning.

"Give me children, or I shall die!" Rachel once yelled at her husband, Jacob, after she watched his other wife—her sister, Leah—give birth to one son after another. Her plea enraged Jacob, who responded in kind: "Am I in the place of God, who has withheld from you the fruit of the womb?" (Gen. 30:1–2). Hardly our finest moment, ladies and gentlemen. In our theology, it is easy to gloss over the enmity that so often followed in the wake of barrenness. But to struggle with infertility is, in some sense, to peer behind the curtain and face the full magnitude of our biological, emotional, and relational brokenness.

It is not an Orthodox teaching that childlessness (or any bodily blight) is the direct punishment for sin, generational or otherwise. Instead, it seems that God allows certain couples into this dimension of His love for mankind, the side of His love that calls out to our emptiness, just as He allows other couples to perceive His love through abundance and procreation—or monastics to do so through the death of celibacy. I don't know why this is the case, but I do know that nothing has communicated to me the wonder of God's loving, creative act more clearly than this desert of infertility. Every month that passes without a pregnancy, I bear in my body something, if only a faint echo, of humanity's distance from "the mark" of true fellowship with God. Most of the time, I find this too frustrating, too sad, to wax poetic about. But there have been other times, brief moments, when this knowledge has seemed "too wonderful" for me (Ps. 139:6, NRSV), because it reminds me of all God has done in bringing us closer to Him out of our oblivion.

Still, barrenness is not a comfortable truth. If we are to glean only one thing from Adam and Eve, perhaps it is the importance of recognizing the seeds of fragmentation in our lives before they become fully formed rifts. Infertility may be difficult to face as a couple, but thankfully the "law of fragmentation" we've just explored is only one dynamic that holds sway in our lives—only one side of a story that ends not with death and dissolution but with life everlasting.

❧

"It was hard when loved ones gave me the impression that they feared that my marriage or my family life would be doomed without children because I was already struggling to overcome that fear in myself!" —Teresa

❧

"I married an only son in the family, so the pressure to have kids to carry on the family name is constant and has made me fight with my spouse about what a failure our marriage is without kids." —Adrienne

❧

WHAT'S LEFT UNSAID

"Seriously, what was Joachim *thinking*?" I have asked my husband roughly twenty-one times by now, storming into whatever he happens to be in the middle of. We have talked in circles and circles about Joachim and his flight to the desert. Was it a holy thing to do or just insensitive? But it couldn't have been insensitive because he was a *saint*.

My husband is of the tongue-in-cheek opinion that the desert was a kind of pious second-century equivalent of the mancave. "But Joachim wasn't going there to get away from Anna. He was trying to fix the problem the only way he knew how—by praying," he explains. More than that, he points out, Joachim was willing to die in the process—the wilderness was not just a place where people prayed or sorted themselves out, it was also a place where they could easily succumb to the spiritual and natural elements. It is "the home of despair," as the Catholic monastic Thomas Merton described in his *Thoughts in Solitude*. "[T]he man who wanders into the desert to be himself must take care that he does not go mad and become the servant of the [evil] one who dwells there in a sterile paradise of emptiness and rage." Eventually, my husband and I wind up at the same place every time we have this discussion: Joachim's fasting for God to open Anna's womb was, in its own way, loving and self-sacrificial.

But that's not truly the issue. I never had a problem with Joachim *going* to the desert. What rattles my nerves is a scant, ten-word clause (see italics): "And Joachim was exceedingly grieved, *and did not come into the presence of his wife.*" Joachim didn't *just* go pray in the desert, he ghosted Anna in the process. Even the narrator seems baffled and wants us to know that this is not okay, even by the standards of late antiquity. We are supposed to be unsettled.

"I have always used work and vocation as my sense of purpose, which is not the case with my wife. Since we grieved differently and even began with a different understanding of our purpose there was a tension, especially as the years went by and we continued to experience infertility." —Aaron

In the Church, it is tempting to gloss over the actual humanity of saints—their weaknesses, their needs, their infirmities, their relationships. It's almost as though, for their lives to have been truly valid testimonies of Christ, we must scour their memory of any fault (or personality) whatsoever. The older I get, the less instructive I find this mode of piety. Only Christ was without sin. What makes saints' lives edifying is not so much that they managed to stay on the path effortlessly and without exception, but that they managed to come *back* to the path—again, and again, and again, through all that tempted them away from it. And all that coming back sifted them, purified their hearts of sin and self-focus.

This is what brings me hope, because it means that even (and especially) people with blatant, serious struggles can encounter Christ and lead holy lives. So I'll risk some honesty here: I don't think Joachim's trek to the desert was *just* a testament to his faith. It was also a testament to his brokenness, his shame, and maybe even his forgetfulness. And you know what? When I stop trying to explain that facet of Joachim's life away, when I step back and see him as a real person—a man who was so ashamed of himself he could not even show his face to the woman on this earth who loved him most—I am amazed. He managed, with that kind of shame, to turn to God. And God listened.

And what about Anna? Why didn't she bother looking for Joachim or sending someone out for him? Why is she so hasty to identify herself as a widow? Her twofold lament is a curious one, considering that just a few scenes later, she will offer up her own prayers to God for a child (clearly she had some inkling Joachim wasn't actually dead). Perhaps widowhood was the only vocabulary she had to adequately express how dark and deserted she felt—by Joachim, yes, but also by God, by life. As socially and economically precarious as widowhood was in Anna's day, it at least came with a kind of script. There were things you did, items you wore, ways you were expected to act. There isn't a corollary script for grieving barrenness. For all its shame and stigma, the claim to widowhood was a way to categorize an otherwise tenuous, enigmatic situation.

I guess what I'm saying is that more than anything that is said in this section of the *Protoevangelium*, I am troubled by what is left unsaid. I suppose what Catholic theologian Pierre Grelot once wrote of husband-wife relationships in Scripture is also applicable here: "We shouldn't expect to find . . . an analysis of the human couple such as is given by modern writers" nor a "detailed psychological examination of passionate love, as our playwrights and novelists do." What we are given instead is an account that goes beyond the "fragmentation" of psychoanalysis, with its bare mechanics and instincts, and offers a narrative capable of integrating these disparate pieces. This narrative is none other than "that of the relationship of [a] human couple with the living God."[36]

Despite my wishes to the contrary, the text refuses to pull back the curtain on the full extent of the marital and emotional complexity of this scene. It's a powerful reminder that the separation of a man and woman is in some ways just as much a mystery as their union forged in holy matrimony. When a marriage begins to fall apart, even just a little bit, there is always more at work—more pain, more confusion, more subtext—than what can be expressed in words. The gaps, the unanswered questions, the understated details—our own confusion as readers parallels the disconnect unfolding between Joachim and Anna, thrusting us into the center of their disorienting, isolating turmoil.

∞

"Infertility grief never completely goes away. For me, the loss was originally a nightmare that only began to fade when I found other outlets for my maternal feelings. A second wave of grief resurfaced when I reached grandmother age."
—*Michaela*

DOES INFERTILITY CAUSE SEPARATION?
SIX RISK FACTORS

For a long time, it was assumed, even among experts, that marriages touched by infertility were automatically more likely to end in divorce (up to two or three times the average, depending on which article or study you consulted). In the last five or ten years, however, more nuanced research has begun to show that infertility is likely not the only factor responsible for marital breakdown.

Instead, it seems that infertility can have either a positive or negative effect on a marriage, depending on how the couple approaches it. On the negative side, it can activate or intensify certain risk factors that eventually lead to marital dissatisfaction. I believe it is beneficial for all couples facing infertility to be aware of these factors, even if their marriage is not currently at risk. The tricky thing about infertility is that it can last a long time, and the stress associated with it creeps up gradually over the course of months or years. Having these items on your mutual radar as a couple helps you stay proactive and intentional.

In my personal reading and informal interviews with others, six risk factors for marital breakdown in couples with infertility surfaced most frequently.

"My wife and I both went into marriage wanting a big family. After we lost our first child and then couldn't conceive, it was hard because we thought we might have to adjust to a very different kind of life." —Gregory

RISK FACTOR #1: A lack of meaningful communication, mutual respect, and/or trust between husband and wife

Facing infertility well as a couple requires a foundation of communication, respect, and trust. For some couples, there are cracks in this bedrock before they even start trying to have kids, and these cracks are intensified when children are harder to conceive than expected. But the sensitive nature of infertility and the situations or conversations it prompts can destabilize even the healthiest marriages. While not all the risk factors on this list necessitate seeking outside or professional help, in this instance enlisting the support of a couples therapist, skilled priest, or trusted third party to help strengthen the foundation of your marriage is recommended—and sooner rather than later.

RISK FACTOR #2: Unresolved shame, guilt, anger, or sadness in one or both spouses with regard to their lack of children

Sometimes the emotional intensity of our grief, as distinct from infertility per se, can itself become a source of distress and isolation. When emotional pain inhibits our ability to participate in daily life or relationships for a prolonged period, we should pay attention. Maybe we need to have a good cry, talk with a friend, see a doctor, or make an appointment with a counselor. Other times, as trite as it sounds, we might just need an excuse to distract ourselves or "snap out of it" for a while. This is not meant to minimize the reality of deep pain, but speaking as someone who is highly sensitive to emotions, giving myself permission to be happy once in a while, or neutral at the very least, is sometimes more beneficial than some huge catharsis or therapy session. Only you can determine what you need to reconnect.

"*I became very depressed because of our infertility, and that put stress on my marriage.*" —Kristen

RISK FACTOR #3: Different or misunderstood coping strategies partners use to manage infertility stress

We've already established in this book that everyone *grieves* differently, but we also *cope* with that grief differently. Some individuals have a confrontative coping style that moves them toward others, social support, and the source of pain. Others have a distancing coping style that moves them away from others and the source of pain. A 2006 study on the impact of infertility stress found that these differences in coping styles are often tied to gender: "Women used proportionately greater amounts of confrontative coping, accepting responsibility, seeking social support and escape/avoidance when compared with men, whereas men used proportionately greater amounts of distancing, self-controlling and planful problem-solving."[37]

While there is no right or wrong way to cope (all coping styles can be applied in healthy and less healthy ways), it is not uncommon for tension, misunderstanding, and harsh dynamics to result when each spouse tends toward a different coping style. Curiosity, openness, and empathy help bring things back to a middle ground. Instead of asking why your spouse *doesn't* deal with their grief the way you'd like them to or think they should, you might ask (in a spirit of compassionate curiosity) why they *do* deal with it the way they do. What drives them toward or away from you, what thoughts do they wrestle with, how does their coping style help them? Finding ways to talk openly and without criticism about styles of coping can open new pathways of learning and understanding within a marriage.

"*To manage the emotional aspects of infertility, I threw
myself more into my work for my sense of masculinity.
I am not a handyman, nor a mechanic, etc. Without
having children, I made my work my focus, my sense of
accomplishment and providing for my 'family.' I most
assuredly did this to an unhealthy and workaholic degree.*"
—*Aaron*

**RISK FACTOR #4: The stress of long-term cycle monitoring
and scheduled intimacy**
Need I say more? Nothing kills the mood more quickly than ovulation tracking and copulation hacking, especially when it's all permeated by the nagging sense that something is wrong with your
bod(ies). As one literature review said of couples with infertility,
"Problems associated with sexual pleasure appeared to be due to
the mechanical and forced sexual activities for conception purposes,
which included scheduled post-coital tests, and the optimal states for
sexual intercourse during the female ovulatory period." (Just *reading*
that is like the verbal equivalent of a cold shower, to say nothing of
actually experiencing some of these factors.)

It takes effort to keep charting and counting days, but it takes even
more work to maintain a sense of play, desire, and freedom when it
comes to intimacy in infertility—a challenge that we ironically share
with the vast majority of young parents out there. Perhaps this is
why many who took the *Under the Laurel Tree Questionnaire* empha-
sized the need to take breaks from actively trying to conceive. I like
to think of these breaks as Sabbath months—times set apart not so

much from sex itself, but from the scheduled, pressure-laden "work" of trying to conceive. Cover up the calendar once in a while and go on dates, be relaxed, and forget about The Plan. Just as God rested on the seventh day, Sabbath months provide times to sit back, behold, and remember that it—your partner, your life together, your shared intimacy—is (still) good.

⚥

"*Trying to conceive month after month, year after year, nearly broke us.*" —*Michaela*

⚥

"*The pressure of infertility made sex only about procreation. It became a job. This started to pull us apart because even a primal physical connection was extremely difficult to spontaneously have with one another. We had to stop and say let's take a break from tracking ovulation windows and pretend we're dating again.*" —*Sophia*

⚥

RISK FACTOR #5: Disagreements about fertility treatment (broadly defined), adoption, and other "next steps"
Many couples struggle to agree on what, if anything, to do after they learn of their infertility. Even if they share similar religious and social values, one never really knows what one will prefer or be comfortable with until one is in this position—and even then, a person's thoughts after one year of infertility might not stay the same for the three (or ten, or more) years of waiting that lie ahead. Be patient with one another and remember that you're both on the same team;

differences of opinion can deepen the conversation and fine-tune the decision-making process. When in doubt, consult with others—doctors, priests, social workers, family members (at your own risk)—to help navigate a path forward that both spouses can feel comfortable with.

RISK FACTOR #6: The logistical, financial, and emotional strain associated with fertility treatment, particularly when it does not result in pregnancy

Despite being last on the list, this is actually one of the biggest and most research-supported risk factors to pay attention to. Failed infertility treatment—especially, but not limited to, IVF—ranks among the biggest precursors to divorce among infertile couples. Couples counseling before and after treatment can offset this risk factor to some degree, as can learning ahead of time about the limitations of medical interventions for infertility. The lesson here is not so much to shun medical treatment at all costs, but to simply be aware that the risks involved are not just medical, physical, or financial—there can be relational costs, as well. Prepare yourself and your marriage accordingly.

In addition to risk factors, I mentioned at the beginning of this section that infertility can also have a positive effect on marriage. This is particularly true when couples approach it as a team and view it not as a stamp of failure on their marriage but as an opportunity to learn and grow. I had only begun realizing this when I first started writing this book. Until then, I assumed that infertility automatically put my marriage at a disadvantage—that getting through this desert with *us* still intact was akin to constantly beating back a forest fire that at any moment could swallow this precious relationship whole, which is exhausting. Leaning into this topic in my writing awakened me to all the tiny ways this struggle has enriched my relationship with my husband. Some who took the *Under the Laurel Tree Questionnaire* had similar experiences. What we all appear to have in common, and what I firmly believe is the single biggest predictor of marital satisfaction in infertility, is the ability to create and maintain a shared sense of purpose as a couple that doesn't rely solely on children.

"My husband and I were never able to have children of our own. Because of this, we faced bigger and deeper issues earlier in our marriage as we struggled to find meaning and joy in our lives together. Many of our arguments and frustrations then were coming from a place of grief and, at times, boredom. Slowly we learned to make changes, learning activities we enjoy and look forward to, and finding ways to serve. Now some of our friends who did have children are becoming empty nesters and are having to learn a lot of the same lessons twenty years later." —Laura

PURPOSE LOST (AND REGAINED)

Expert opinion and anecdotal evidence alike suggest that regaining a shared sense of purpose, as a couple, is an important part of solidifying marriages in the face of infertility. In a 1989 journal article on the effects of infertility on marriage, the loss of goals and purpose was cited among the many intangibles couples with infertility grieve. In a strange way, this also aligns with the story of Joachim and Anna. Prior to Joachim's encounter with Rubim, both husband and wife had a common purpose: honoring God and offering their lives in service of the temple. Like Joachim, tradition holds that Anna attended the temple of God with Joachim, offering prayers, fasting, and bountiful gifts. Even by the anachronistic standards of twenty-first century couples therapy, they were on the right path—they had even managed, in their childlessness, to stake out a common mission that didn't depend on children or the lack thereof. What made Rubim's comment so scathing was that it delegitimized not just Joachim and his identity, but the whole fabric of the shared, God-centered purpose the couple had cultivated over the decades of their marriage.

"When a woman suffers pain and exhaustion during pregnancy or early child rearing, it at least feels goal-oriented and there's an end to look forward to. With infertility, a woman may spend vast amounts of her mental and physical energy in treatment but have nothing to show for it. Her grief isn't simply over the lack of children, it is bound up with the loss of hours and hours poured out to fulfill one's marital vocation and heart's desire." —Brianna

I like to call what couples with infertility go through "early-onset empty nest syndrome." The kids haven't left the nest, they just never showed up in the first place; but the symptoms are the same. As our peers begin having children, we start running out of things to talk about or do with our spouses. We begin to wonder how we'll manage to fill the next two, three, four decades of life and marriage that (Lord willing) stand between us and the grave. As a GPS does after a wrong turn, in long-term infertility a marriage enters a period of "recalculating." While there are countless books to help couples sharpen their communication and listening skills, far fewer tackle the need to establish a common purpose in marriage, even though this is arguably a more difficult (and vital) task. (Better communication is a lot easier when you enjoy your time together and sense your future has meaning and purpose.) Without a shared vision, what are you supposed to *do* and *enjoy together* with all those "I statements" and active listening skills?

My husband and I once decided to see a counselor for a challenge we were facing. When we went to schedule our first appointment with the therapist, the only available timeslot was during the same week we were to begin improv comedy lessons (improv was on both our bucket lists, so we took the plunge together). That first session with the counselor was draining; we spent the entire drive home arguing. On the flip side, later in the week we spent the ride home from our first comedy class laughing and teasing each other. Sometimes working toward a common goal—even after just one evening—does more to bolster togetherness than the best talk therapy. Sharing the fear, nerves, and awkwardness of our first comedy class felt like a huge accomplishment as a couple. It helps that improv comedy just happens to be the most hilarious way to spend a weekday evening.

❧

"*I think infertility and recurrent miscarriage has made our marriage rock-solid. We have turned to one another, so many times, in our grief and sadness, and just thanked God for one another. I expect we might have more practice at this than some of our friends who haven't experienced so much*

*pregnancy loss. Also our home is much quieter and focused,
which means our family relationships are quite intense. There
isn't quite as much hustle and bustle to distract us from
one another. I would definitely say that we experience both
pressure and a very intense sense of purpose in our marriage."*
—Teresa

Shared goals and purposes come in all shapes and sizes. A simple
place to start is establishing one or more rituals of connection as a
couple—routines that foster regular connection, such as waking up
or going to sleep together, kissing each other goodbye in the morning
or hello after work, going for a walk after dinner, scheduling a weekly
date night, or at the end of each day sharing three things you are
grateful for. From there, maybe you move on to brainstorming bigger, more long-term hopes and dreams: trips to take, ways to serve,
languages to learn, places to explore. Terry Gaspard of the renowned
Gottman Institute notes, "When couples have [a] shared dream, the
inevitable ups and downs of marriage are less bothersome. Creating
a larger context of meaning in life can help couples to avoid focusing
only on the little stuff that happens and to keep their eyes on the big
picture." I'm not sure the loss associated with infertility automatically gets "less bothersome" when you find new dreams to dream
together, but there is at least a sense that life is moving forward in a
meaningful and positive way rather than stagnating.

Establishing these kinds of shared dreams and purposes takes
time and effort. I have been thinking about this because the Christian nonprofit I work for recently approved a new mission statement.
I think it's the first time it's been revised in decades, and it took
months and months of discussion, planning, committee meetings,

and consensus-building to make it happen. The organization even managed to distill this vision statement down into a three-keyword tagline to focus and clarify its purpose on letterhead, email signatures, and so forth.

Like any organization, every marriage has a mission, and sometimes you have to step back and reclarify that mission when times or circumstances change, or you lose your sense of direction. Dwight D. Eisenhower reputedly said, "In preparing for battle I have always found that plans are useless, but planning is indispensable." Something similar is true in developing a mission in marriage. The act of coming to the table in the heat of struggle to plan and envision a way forward together—and actively taking steps in that direction—is almost more important than what your goals are or whether you accomplish every bullet point on the list.

∞

"My husband and I have been married 45 years. Strange as it sounds, dealing with infertility 30 years ago gave us a common goal. Working together on trying to get pregnant helped us work together on other things later, like starting and running a business together and dealing with the death of a child 10 years ago." —Dorothy

∞

REINTEGRATION IN AN UNLIKELY WAY

Around the time my husband and I realized we were dealing with infertility, we found ourselves in Greece on vacation. An Orthodox physician at our church recommended we visit a particular convent where many couples struggling to get pregnant have experienced healing. We arrived in time for vespers, the beautiful voices of the nuns echoing from the centuries-old chapel and flowing down the rural hillside under a vibrant Greek sunset. It had been only hours since we stepped off the plane, and I let the calm of their singing soothe my jet lag and culture shock.

After the service, my husband found the abbess and began speaking to her in Greek. I'd never asked for supplications at a monastery before and found myself somewhat nervous to discuss such a sensitive topic with a total stranger. But as my husband translated, the blue-eyed abbess turned to me with a calm, fervent compassion that was immediately disarming. She took my hands and led me to a quiet corner of the chapel.

All at once, she began pulling large human bones from a canister—a femur, I believe, and most of a skull. I gasped. I'm all for relics, but until then I had only encountered them as tiny fragments in ornate cases, where it was easy to overlook the fact that relics are, well, *relics*. The things the abbess presented to us, though, were *real bones*, from *real bodies*, just out in the open. I glanced at my husband quizzically but followed along as he venerated the relics as though it were the most natural thing in the world to do. And then, before I knew it, the abbess was pressing the bones right up against my lower abdomen. It took me a few moments to realize she was praying, first silently and then out loud in Greek.

I stood there, aghast at the sight of a human skull against my womb—a visual oxymoron. As her prayer continued, I came to understand she was dealing with much more than dry bones and a barren womb. She was gathering everything and all creation out of its separated compartments—birth and death, health and infirmity, hope and despair, me and my husband, prayers and longings—and offering them all up to God in the palms of her hands.

Infertility can leave a bitter taste in a person's life. It is the death we never asked for but can't escape: the death of the myth that we are in control of our bodies, the death of thinking we can plan a family on our own terms, the death of the fantasy that we can choose our future. And all those deaths, if we aren't careful, will send shards of bitter brokenness down into the core of our being. Or, if we let them, they will open us up and undo the divisions and enmity we've stored up in these long years of being human.

Several weeks after the monastery visit, I became pregnant and quickly lost the baby. It was, so far as I'm aware, the first and only time I have conceived. In the years since, as I've mourned that loss and the broader grief of infertility, I've traveled many times back to those fleeting yet eternal moments with the abbess. The soft pressure of skull on stomach, her barely audible supplications in the tomb of my ears. And I can't, for the life of me, figure out which was the greater miracle: that her supplications opened my womb just long enough to know what it was to bear another life inside me; or that, for as long as I stood in that paradox beside her, together before God, I got to be—uniquely, undeniably, wholly—who I am.

"What people need to understand is that being childless doesn't make a person sad. It drowns you in agony, pushing you down, not letting you up for air. The pain is all consuming and is accompanied with intense feelings of longing, despair, sadness, anger, frustration, guilt, and loneliness. These feelings can be so utterly overwhelming! I felt like I was dying inside sometimes." —Bethany

"AND THE GREAT DAY OF THE LORD WAS AT HAND": WHY TIME DOES NOT WAIT FOR GRIEF

The section of the *Protoevangelium* we have been dealing with in this chapter cuts off with an awkward, almost jarring non sequitur. Immediately following Anna's outpouring of sorrow, we are randomly informed that "The great day of the Lord was at hand." It is not the first time we have heard this—the great day of the Lord was also at hand back in the first scene of the *Protoevangelium*, when Joachim was in the temple. It's not clear which particular holy day these verses are referring to—some have made the argument for Sukkot, the Jewish Festival of Tabernacles in autumn, but nothing conclusive appears in the text. In a sense, this "day of the Lord" functions as a symbolic leitmotif, a phrase that occurs and recurs like a heartbeat throughout the story. To me, it represents not one festival in particular, but the passage of time in general—the callous audacity of it to keep going, to keep cycling forth, even as we struggle to keep going ourselves.

Wherever we are on the continuum of grief, wherever our marriages presently reside in the liminal space between unity and disconnect, the great day of the Lord never ceases to be at hand for all of us. God is always there, and always moving us into and through, downward and upward, through every cross and every tomb, "through every sigh of [our] sorrow," and on to every moment of new life (Akathist of Thanksgiving, Ikos 1).

Sometimes the "day of the Lord" that shows up is a literal feast day, one that manages—like the Feast of the Nativity of the Theotokos I mentioned in the Introduction—to reveal the mysterious intersections between our personal griefs and the narrative arc of salvation. Other times, these "great days" appear in even less comfortable forms: a call from friends to announce they are pregnant with baby number three (I'll have what she's having, God!), the arrival of yet another childless Christmas season, or another birthday—one more withdrawal from our dwindling bank account of childbearing years. On still other occasions, we are met in our predicament by truly great days—new, unequivocally good times and opportunities that seem to keep coming our way, despite how lowly we feel.

But what all these events teach us, again and again, is that time will never stop for us. We may want it to, especially as those late thirties and early forties loom on the horizon, but it won't. And there will be moments when this reality seems cruel and sinister, but there will also be moments when the clouds of pain clear enough to remember how true it is that all things transpire for good. As I've put it elsewhere, "Where there is time and change, there is the possibility for transformation. . . . Creation was fashioned in such a way that we are never stranded within our worst selves forever."[38] Neither, I would add, are we stranded within our worst situations or feelings. If we allow Him, God will use time to transform us, our partners, our circumstances—maybe not in the way we specifically asked for, but He will jostle and polish our plight until the light of His countenance again shines into our darkness and we can see the next step.

In the case of Joachim and Anna, we will see that time changes them, too. It will bring them to the end of themselves; it will wind up the scroll of Joachim's forty days; it will give them the grace of reconciliation.

But we haven't gotten there yet—we must let time take us where it will. And where it will take us first is deeper into Anna's despair.

DISCUSSION AND REFLECTION QUESTIONS

1. What do you find most surprising or meaningful about this scene of the *Protoevangelium*? What did you learn from Joachim and Anna in this chapter?

2. What do the words *separation* and *reintegration* mean to you in the context of infertility?

3. How has infertility shaped the story you tell yourself or others about your marriage, for better or for worse? In what ways does or doesn't this leave room for the redemption and hope that are found in Christ?

4. In what ways does infertility put pressure on your marriage? By the same token, in what ways has it enriched or strengthened your marriage?

5. What are some purposes, goals, or rituals—no matter how small—you share with your spouse? What are some purposes, goals, or rituals you would *like* to share with your spouse?

CHAPTER 6

Anger

[A]nd Judith her maid-servant said: How long do you humiliate your soul? Behold, the great day of the Lord is at hand, and it is unlawful for you to mourn. But take this head-band, which the woman that made it gave to me; for it is not proper that I should wear it, because I am a maid-servant, and it has a royal appearance. And Anna said: Depart from me; for I have not done such things, and the Lord has brought me very low. I fear that some wicked person has given it to you, and you have come to make me a sharer in your sin. And Judith said: Why should I curse you, seeing that the Lord has shut your womb, so as not to give you fruit in Israel?
—PROTOEVANGELIUM OF JAMES 2

*W*hile Joachim passes his time in the desert, the narrative zooms in on Anna and her grief. Consolation, or at least a bizarre attempt at it, arrives in the form of a headband. That's right: just when the familial fabric of Anna's life has been ripped apart at the seams— her husband is gone, she has no offspring to care for her as she approaches old age—instead of listening to Anna's pain, her servant tries to placate her with a *hair accessory*. To make matters worse,

Anna suspects the headband to be a token of evil deeds (theft? prostitution? witchcraft?). She refuses to wear it, lest she become a participant in Judith's sin. Whether it is issued in defense or just plain cruelty, Judith's response is a low blow: why should she bother cursing Anna, seeing as God had already done a pretty good job of it by "shutting" her womb, "so as not to give [her] fruit in Israel." *Ouch.*

At first glance, this scene is as bizarre as it is enraging. What exactly does the headband represent? What made Anna so angry about it? What was Judith's problem? While the full subtext isn't entirely clear, when we peel away the layers, we find the blueprints of a grievance all too familiar to many childless people: unsolicited, judgmental advice. Failing to grasp the full magnitude of Anna's grief, Judith encourages her to get over it and move on. So she gives Anna some guidance—*wear this headband. It will help.* Anna's sudden anger ("Depart from me!") is driven not merely by the suspicious hairpiece, but also by the more obvious reality that now is hardly the time for such a trivial request ("The Lord has brought me very low").

This chapter delves into the role of anger in grieving infertility, particularly with regard to intrusive and hurtful advice. We may not be confronted by potentially demonic headbands, but who among us hasn't been told to "just adopt," or be thankful, pray more, go on vacation, do acupuncture, or jump through some other hoop to prove to others our dedication to Project Pregnancy? On the ever-accelerating treadmill of fertility advice and social pressure, our efforts never seem adequate in the eyes of certain people—there will always be another miraculous monastery someone thinks we should try, another fertility diet we need to subject ourselves to if our struggle is finally to be deemed legitimate.

In the face of intrusive advice, anger becomes a daily struggle and, with time, hardens into resentment. Why is unsolicited advice such a stumbling block in this form of grief? How can we deal with

the anger these suggestions trigger in a way that is meaningful and
life-giving?

"*Many conversations with other parishioners (particularly
women) contain a lot of what I assume has been well-meaning
advice. Suggestions that particular relics, saints, or rituals are
the key to solving barrenness are actually quite hurtful. The
implied message is that I am missing something, or simply
going about things the wrong way. It conveys fault. Indeed,
even the assurance from friends that this is 'God's will' or
'God's plan' can be tremendously hurtful. In the beginning of
our journey with infertility, I grasped onto these suggestions
with (what I now realize) was the hope that I could control or
manipulate God into blessing us with children. But that is a
kind of magical thinking.*" —Emilia

THE PROBLEM WITH ADVICE

No matter where we are or what we're doing, it seems, we're never
very far from our next "headband from a handmaiden" moment.
Whether we're talking about a recent doctor appointment or setback
on the fertility front, or whether we're saying nothing at all—just
trying to blend into a group conversation at work or church—unsolicited advice has a way of finding us, and usually when we're at our
weakest. It can be given in a variety of forms: loaded questions, mat-
ter-of-fact remarks, vague allusions to possible reasons for or (solutions to) our misfortune. And while it may not be the only source

of anger for those facing infertility, it is certainly one of the most frustrating.

The vast majority of female participants in the *Under the Laurel Tree Questionnaire* listed fertility-related advice as a major source of stress. When asked what the Church could do to better support people grieving infertility, the top answer was to simply listen and be present instead of offering suggestions or solutions. Dana says, "I've been told by my family members that I need to lose weight or eat fewer carbs or cut out gluten to have children. People tell me to relax, or try harder, or be 'more open' (what does that mean?). No one asks how I'm *doing* with this." Dorothy feels "the biggest problem in the Church, when one is facing a challenge like this, is that people pretend the challenge isn't there. They judge and talk about the person behind their back, and give un-asked-for advice, instead of JUST LISTENING."

Why exactly is unsolicited advice so infuriating? Because no matter how loving or thoughtful it may be, it is inherently "othering"; it underscores the chasm between us and those around us. Just when we are most in need of connection and compassion, advice provides a vehicle for others to position themselves as authority (or judgment) figures rather than true co-sufferers. Whether intentionally or not (and most of the time it is not), unrequested advice communicates the message that others know our situation—and how to fix it—better than we do.

It also sends the message that no matter what we are doing or who we are outside of our struggle with infertility, we must fix this problem before we are worthy of true fellowship with others. Countless times, I have found myself in group gatherings where the topic of conversation has nothing to do with children or childbearing; then out of nowhere, someone turns to me and tells me how their aunt (or sister, or mother) couldn't get pregnant until she said a particular prayer or adopted a certain diet. *Does my infertility bother people so much that they have to derail an entire conversation to address it?* I've wondered. It's enough to make me avoid social gatherings altogether, at least when I know other women will be there (men, bless their hearts, are either too squeamish or too considerate even to think of advising a lady about her empty womb).

Most of us understand intuitively that it would be cruel to suggest to someone who is terminally ill or had lost a child tragically that they could have done something differently to avoid their predicament. Yet, in infertility, it is almost socially acceptable to make suggestions like this—perhaps because we don't recognize it first and foremost as a source of grief. We approach it instead as a problem to be solved, a code to be cracked, a curse to be broken. As a result, we fail to see the damage that even seemingly harmless comments like "just pray!" can do. Even spiritual-sounding and well-intentioned advice like this implies that the reason someone is not pregnant is because they *haven't* been praying—or haven't been praying hard enough, long enough, sincerely enough.

Earlier, I asked why receiving advice is so difficult. The more perplexing question to me, though, is why people feel the need to give advice in the first place. On my forgiving days, I can see that giving advice is one way for others to sidestep the feelings of powerlessness I must wrestle with every day. Ultimately this perpetuates the myth that with a little knowledge, prayer, or magical thinking, we can control a situation that by all other accounts is untamable. Tasking me with something to do offers others an explanation—however unfounded—for why I'm childless. My situation is not just random chaos or an unfathomable tragedy, it's somehow the direct result of something I've done or not done. If they could just find the cause—whether it's physical, spiritual, or even sexual—they could fix me and return to their comfortable faith in a God who never visits us with hardships, at least not ones that can't be managed, concealed, or hacked.

Oops, I forgot I was talking about my forgiving days. Which brings me to my (many) cynical days, when all I can see in people's advice is a patronizing, parental power dynamic. Why is it we so often view suffering people as enfeebled and incompetent? This seems to happen particularly often with infertility—in some people's eyes, it's as though my lack of children makes me a child myself, one who must be taught, prodded, and interrogated on the hardest, most difficult aspect of my life. As though I haven't already researched everything about fertility I could get my hands on from the moment I realized we would be unable to conceive easily. As though I haven't scoured my memories and secret sins, like a desperate search for worms hiding beneath the heavy stones of my life, wondering what forgotten iniquity God must be punishing me for. As though I haven't prayed, visited monasteries, gone to confession, received Holy Unction, avoided junk food, seen doctors, taken tests, counted days . . .

I have. We all have, in our own way. Not everyone is dealing with infertility, but we all have that one tragedy in our lives that refuses to follow all the rules or adhere to the plan. The sooner we acknowledge that, the sooner we quit the advice and fault-finding, the sooner we learn to see ourselves (and Christ) in one another, the sooner we will learn to stand with one another in the helplessness that points us to God.

∞

"When someone is struggling with this issue, don't hand them the card to a fertility specialist. On the other hand, don't start telling them all the things that they can't do in light of Church doctrines. Just listen. Make sure that the Church is a

safe place where people can be vulnerable about their genuine struggles and their needs." —Aaron

TIME AND SHAME: THE LAYERS OF ANGER

Most of the time, anger is not a primary but a secondary emotion, a way of disguising other, more painful feelings, typically shame. "Shame is so painful," says Fr. Stephen Freeman in his pivotal talk "Orthodoxy and Shame," "that rather than face it, we change it to anger." When someone has angered us, it most often means they have shamed us. It is easier to dwell in the self-aggrandizement of anger than in the inadequacy and isolation of shame. Healthy anger, Fr. Stephen continues, "is a gift from God. It is a very short emotion. It gives a burst of energy. Anger can help you lift a car off your uncle, toss a piano. . . . But if you've been angry for more than a few minutes, it's not normal anger. There's something else that's energizing it. And usually what's energizing it is shame."[39]

Time is the litmus test that differentiates true anger from its dark underbelly of shame. As I reflect on the last few years of infertility, I can vividly recall comments that still raise my blood pressure in fury. Now, I recognize that these same interactions touched the nerve of my limitation and perceived unworthiness, my emptiness and vulnerability, as a person without children. I know the anger is driven not by a neutral concern for injustice, but by the sense of having my shame exposed.

If shame is the inner kernel of anger, resentment is its hardened exoskeleton. Living in Canada, we know it's been a cold winter when, on rare occasions, the Niagara Falls freeze completely. The news channels fill with pictures of its giant, razor-sharp icicles, a once-roaring current now petrified into unmoving shards of ice. This, I think, is an icon of resentment—frozen, rock-hard rage that, while more subdued than raw anger, is ultimately paralyzed and paralyzing.

Again, time functions as the delineating factor. When the unresolved anger of grief festers, it calcifies into resentment. Fr. Anthony Coniaris states:

> Some people say that the greatest cure for grief is time. Yet, by itself time will not heal grief completely. Time can also make grief worse. Time can turn grief into bitter resentment that can poison the body and the mind. In order to grieve properly and heal the pain of loss, we must cooperate with time in ways that are constructive.[40]

The first step of "cooperating with time," I think, is being honest about our anger, first and foremost with ourselves. To ignore or put a friendly face on it is to allow anger to do its damage silently and below the radar, slowly hardening us from the inside out.

"I wish that people would get that infertility causes anger and that no matter how hard a person tries to hide it and ignore it and make it go away, it doesn't. We need understanding and compassion for these intense feelings."
—Bethany

ANGER AND GRIEF

Before infertility, I would not have considered myself an angry person. Headstrong, impatient, and driven, yes. Insecure and prone to thinly veiled passive aggression, perhaps. But true anger—fiery, impassioned, raw—would have violated the seemingly sacred code of conduct I was born into as a native of the Midwest, where displays of emotion threaten the sturdy crust of repression that for generations has fortified us against the injustice of Wisconsin winters. But child-lessness changed all that. Until then, every struggle I'd faced seemed vaguely fair—a reasonable allotment of suffering proportionate to my age, weight, and perceived degree of sinfulness. Infertility, by contrast, exceeded my concept of fairness so much that it fractured my veneer of calm, tinting my life with a dark, silently churning rage.

Suddenly, I saw my circumstances as a balance sheet, a scorecard of ways life had failed to deliver on what some insistent part of me felt I was entitled to. I couldn't shake the sense that life—and most people in it—owed me. Anger crept into the mundane trials of daily interactions—a long line at the grocery store, a tedious conversation with a relative, a personal slight blown out of proportion. These now became further signs of how frustratingly little I could ask of reality. I had, as Evagrius Ponticus wrote in the fourth century, made myself and perhaps others a "fugitive" to my anger. "If this should happen your whole life long," he writes, "you will yourself not be able to flee from the demon of sadness."[41]

Among the stages of grief, anger is perhaps the most unex-pected—at least for someone like me, who for most of her life assumed she was a stranger to it. But maybe I was kidding myself all along. How much of my longsuffering demeanor has consisted not of true patience but of concealed anger, wrestled into a straitjacket somewhere deep inside?

Fr. Thomas Hopko distinguished between two kinds of anger: godly anger, the kind that afflicts saints and other holy people in the face of true injustice or spiritual warfare, and ungodly anger,

> the anger that comes when we're just not getting our own way, the anger when we feel offended, or the anger when people treat us badly, or the anger when we are not praised or pitied or whatever we want

from people; anger when our material or carnal needs are not satis-fied. . . . Or we could be angry over our own life, angry over the way things are with us.[42]

If I'm honest, there is much about my infertility anger that resem-bles this description. But then I remember St. Paul's surprising com-mand to the Ephesians: "be angry, and do not sin" (Eph 4:26). He does not say *"when you are angry,"* or *"when you are angry in the cor-rect, godly way, do not sin."* He says, first, to *be* angry, in the impera-tive. Perhaps before one can learn how to be angry without sinning, one must first learn to be angry. To stop kidding ourselves and get on with the business of pursuing holiness, anger and all.

"My four-year-old son once wondered, out loud, in our church, why he didn't have more siblings. A woman told him that he just needed to pray more! It was probably the most hurtful moment in this journey. We've prayed a whole lot, and God has not brought us a child." —Teresa

It took infertility for me to learn to be angry—I mean, *really* angry. Deliciously, indignantly, pridefully angry. Angry not just at God or the abstract situation of infertility, but at people—at their words, their broken attempts to say something helpful in my suffering, their questions, and frankly, at their good fortune sometimes. And that anger awakened me to my self-delusion, showed me that I am not above the sway of strong emotion and impulsivity. My anger, too, revealed subtle myths that had crept into my theology: the fan-tasy that "bad" things don't happen to "good" people, and that (by implication) I thought of myself as a "good person," and that deep down, life is more about getting what I want than it is about learning to pour myself out as an offering of thanks, in the example of Christ.

But just as infertility taught me to be angry, it also helped me recover the desire not to sin in that anger, in the self-righteousness of it. I am still learning what this means, but I think it has something to do with these words from St. John Chrysostom: "Be angry with the devil and not your own member. This is why God has armed us with anger. Not that we should thrust the sword against our own bodies, but that we should baptize the whole blade in the devil's breast."[43] The purpose of anger is to ignite our hatred of the evil one, not our hatred of those around us or of ourselves.

Where is the evil one in infertility? Perhaps not, as one might assume, in the condition of infertility itself, as though it were a curse, but rather in the division, judgmentalism, despair, and malice it so often causes—both in us, as people with infertility, and in those who interact with us. Maybe part of not sinning in anger means learning to shift our enmity away from the people who have hurt us and toward the audacity of the devil, who warps our understanding of one another and of this condition. Sinful anger, St. John also says, "will cause us to suspect that words spoken in one sense were meant in another. And we will even do the same with gestures and every little thing." If we are not careful, we will waste our lives on suspicion and contempt.

These days, I am growing tired of the anger—it has, like a disease, begun to run its course for now. I feel it slipping away, my grip on it loosening. In its place is a kind of peace, a letting of life—and people, their feebleness and my own—off the hook. People are just people. Life is just life. God is just God. And infertility, strange as it sounds, is just infertility. No more, and no less.

❧

"*Those of us who are struggling need to be reminded that regardless of how our fertility journey goes, we can still have a good and full life.*" —Michaela

❧

"*My wish is that hurtful things, well-meaning or not, weren't said, and that people could recognize that I already fear this is somehow my fault. Please believe it is not for my lack of will that I have not borne children. Not my lack of prayers. Not my lack of belief. Not my lack of respect for the Church. The prayers and blessings that exist will continue to exist. The message that God's blessing only comes by the fulfillment of these promises will continue to perpetuate my own dread and fuel the temptation to believe that God does not love me, and extrapolating from that, that He is the kind of God who is stingy with His love. Please do not assist in increasing my own doubt by voicing judgment and criticism.*" —Emilia

❧

BOUNDARIES AND FORGIVENESS: A BALANCING ACT

None of this is to say that dealing with anger in a Christlike way requires that we become pious doormats. Anna, in her fury, passionately renounced the evil Judith had exposed her to in foisting that dubiously procured headband on her. Jesus' words, too, were full of similar wake-up calls, abrupt signals to those around Him that they were crossing a line. "Get behind Me, Satan," He said to Peter (Matt. 16:23). "How long shall I be with you and bear with you?" He sighed when His disciples were unable to heal a demon-possessed boy (Luke 9:41). "[A]re you betraying the Son of Man with a kiss?" He asked Judas as he entered the Garden of Gethsemane (Luke 22:48). For all His lovingkindness, the Son of God was no pushover—He let people know when they were overstepping their bounds instead of allowing them to proceed in their sin unchecked. He knew when to embrace and when to refrain from embracing, when to be firm and when to be gentle. Setting parameters was part of how He demonstrated His love for mankind.

I try to remember this side of Christ—and the example of Anna— when my anger clamors for my attention. So often, the initial flicker of fury is a sign that a boundary has been breached. Ignoring that too often, perhaps in an effort to avoid conflict or please others, does not alleviate the anger but freezes it into resentment. I believe that suppressing anger is a particular temptation for women facing infertility. I once read that those of us with a dearth of children tend to feel less feminine. Out of insecurity, we are more likely to overcompensate for this in subtle ways—by spending more time on our hair and makeup, perhaps, or by displaying more passivity and warmth, qualities modern Western culture has stereotypically associated with femininity. It's bad enough to be a barren woman, still worse to be seen as a cold and crabby one—which we fear we will become if we exhibit any sign of strength, space, or self-respect.

For a long time, I thought it was my job—my unique yoke of martyrdom—to accommodate any and all remarks about my infertility, no matter how ignorant or even rude they were. I smiled agreeably when a professor rejoiced at my plight, since babies would only slow down a writing career. I looked the other way when an acquaintance, curious as to why we hadn't had children yet, asked my husband, "So what's wrong with *her*?" Meaning me, more specifically my obviously deficient womb. I tried to tune out a bishop's homily that extolled parents with children and denigrated couples without kids for their supposedly self-focused and vain lives. Outside, I was smiling as if nothing were wrong; inside, though, I was seething.

Somewhere along the way, I couldn't keep up the ruse—I was being duplicitous, double-minded. My silence, I slowly realized, wasn't a virtue but a variation of hypocrisy, one that allowed me to feign piety and others to continue their unkind and simplistic judgments. Moreover, my misguided martyr complex revealed a cynical rather than loving view of others—avoiding honesty with them showed that deep down, I didn't believe they were capable of remorse or empathy.

Sometimes loving one's neighbor requires a bit of honesty. It may take creativity and patience to determine how (or whether) to speak the truth in love, but it's worth it. Since I began to speak up and share my struggle with those around me, things have begun to change. It's hard to argue with vulnerability. People have (mostly) stopped asking what's wrong with my body and have begun listening to my story, my pain. They've shared with me their own anguish at my situation, and how difficult it is for them to know what to say—and what *not* to say. I've even witnessed a bishop publicly acknowledge how hurtful certain comments he has made could be to those struggling to conceive. Voicing my pain and anger in (I hope) appropriate ways has revealed more humility and understanding in others than my resentful self would once have given them credit for. In all this, harnessing my anger to open up space for greater dialogue has helped me transform bitterness into freedom, forgiveness, and mutual understanding.

"*When we first realized we were struggling with infertility, we made a point of sharing this with several relatives and asked them to keep this news confidential. One relative, a former nurse, seemed to think that it could be solved by stress reduction, even though we knew a medical cause for our infertility. She tried to steer us toward assisted reproduction options we were not interested in pursuing. We later realized she had also told a group of friends about our situation without asking us first. I was extremely angry at the time, but was so exhausted from meds that I just would just try to make the conversation end as soon as possible.*"
—Brianna

CONCLUSION

Whenever the latest storm of anger begins to subside, I am restored by the truth of the Psalmist's words, "What is there in heaven for me but You?" (Ps. 72/73:25). Where the words and actions of man may fail, and where my own heart fails just as often, God's love remains—seeing, embracing, forgiving. It's an unexpected place to find peace, given that the kernel of my pain—childlessness—is something God could conceivably heal at any moment if He wanted to. But with God is healing and comfort, nonetheless. "Though He slay me, yet will I trust in Him," Job once proclaimed (Job 13:15, NKJV)—words I try, rather timidly, to make my own. When I do, even a little, I learn to surrender the world—its shortcomings, the memories of grievances I seem to hoard like coins for a rainy day—to Him who created it. It is not mine to fix or adjudicate; I am only called to tend to my own soul, not to police everyone else's. Sometimes, to do that we have to step back from the crowds as Christ did. We have to know our limits and honor them as the beginning of humility. Like Anna, we have to discern when to depart from the headband-wielding handmaidens of this world and seek solitude under the laurel tree.

DISCUSSION AND REFLECTION QUESTIONS

1. What were your initial impressions of this scene in the *Protoevangelium?*

2. Have you ever had a "headband from a handmaiden" moment? What happened? Would you handle it any differently now than you did then?

3. Why do you think people give advice? Have you ever offered painful or unsolicited advice to someone else that you regret?

4. What role has anger played in shaping your experience of infertility? What would it mean for you to "be angry, and do not sin" (Eph. 4:26)?

5. What have you learned about anger over the course of your life?

CHAPTER 7

Bargaining

And Anna was grieved exceedingly, and put off her garments of mourning, and cleaned her head, and put on her wedding garments, and about the ninth hour went down to the garden to walk. And she saw a laurel, and sat under it, and prayed to the Lord, saying: O God of our fathers, bless me and hear my prayer, as You blessed the womb of Sarah, and gave her a son Isaac.

    And gazing towards the heaven, she saw a sparrow's nest in the laurel, and made a lamentation in herself, saying: Alas! Who begot me? And what womb produced me? Because I have become a curse in the presence of the sons of Israel, and I have been reproached, and they have driven me in derision out of the temple of the Lord. Alas! To what have I been likened? I am not like the fowls of the heaven, because even the fowls of the heaven are productive before You, O Lord. Alas! To what have I been likened? I am not like the beasts of the earth, because even the beasts of the earth are productive before You, O Lord. Alas! To what have I been likened? I am not like these waters, because even these waters are productive before You, O Lord. Alas! To what have I been likened? I

*am not like this earth, because even the earth brings forth its
fruits in season, and blesses You, O Lord.*
PROTOEVANGELIUM OF JAMES, 2–3

If infertility hangs around long enough, something changes: people
stop telling you to pray.

It happens gradually, almost imperceptibly. In the first year or
two, folks will just smile and encourage you to have faith. To them,
your someday baby is little more than a prayer (or oil anointing, or
fasting season) away.

But as the months drag on into years, their smiles grow wearier,
their talk of prayer and miracles more tentative. And then, after one
or two or ten years have gone by, it will happen. You will be mourning yet another failed pregnancy test or fertility treatment, and a
friend will turn to you.

"Maybe it's time to just accept God's will," she will say casu-
ally, as though you had been lamenting the weather. Whatever her
good intentions are, her words will plunge a realization deep into
your sinking stomach: people are slowly giving up. Not everyone,
of course, perhaps not even most people, but enough to make hope
begin to feel irresponsible. Socially awkward.

No one warned me this would happen. I was too worried about
the biological clock to consider that there was a "prayer-ological" one
as well. Evidently, some prayer requests have a shelf life. There is an
arbitrary point in time—regardless of how many childbearing years
God grants these ovaries of mine—when continuing to pray for a
baby becomes a misguided effort.

I used to grow defensive with people I barely knew constantly
haranguing me to pray for a baby, until I realized there is something
worse: people I barely knew *not* constantly haranguing me to pray
for a baby. Because when they were telling me to pray, it meant deep

down they still believed I had a chance. As belittling as the unsolicited advice discussed in the previous chapter can feel, it's when those admonishments and intrusions begin to grow silent that grief reveals its darkest underbelly.

Anna, too, was past her prayerological prime. By the time she makes her way to the laurel tree, she has long surpassed any remotely reasonable time frame for continuing to pray for children—according to pious tradition, she and Joachim had already been married some fifty years. Yet it is only now that her longing reaches its painful pinnacle before God. Instead of delegitimizing her prayers, the long years of anguish only sharpen her supplication.

Echoing numerous Old Testament infertility sagas, Anna's lamentation in the garden challenges our modern, unspoken etiquette of prayer. The God who hears Anna does not seem to favor dignified acceptance or politeness, but rather desperation, pushback, and unrelenting grief—at least when it is offered in faith and virtue. Surely He could have sought a more stoic woman to bear the long-awaited Virgin, but He turns to Anna precisely *after* years (no, decades!) of the same old request. What is more, the prayers of Anna accomplished not just any pregnancy, but one that would bring about the salvation of the world. If ever there were evidence that God honors assertive, almost pathetically long-suffering prayer, it is here, under the laurel tree.

∞

"*I wish more Orthodox could appreciate that 'religious interventions' (e.g. miracle working icons, holy water, myrrh, prayers to saints, etc.) work for some and not others, no matter how hard one prays. More than a 'cure' for infertility, we who are on this journey need to be affirmed that we are not being punished by God. We need to be reminded of Zacharias and Elizabeth, Joachim and Anna."* —Nadia

This chapter reflects on forms of prayer that ask something of God in desperation, even to the point of offering Him something in return. Borrowing more conventional terms, we might refer to this as making vows to the Lord. In the context of grief, though, I prefer to think of it as bargaining with God. In the traditional five stages of grief, bargaining is often depicted as a slightly irrational but somehow necessary part of the grieving process. It involves making promises—to yourself, God, others, the universe—to secure an outcome you don't actually have any control over (e.g., "If my cancer is cured, I'll start going to church again."). It's the stage right before the despair that kicks in after one realizes how futile bargaining can be.

Bargaining often gets a bad rap, both in common understandings (because it seems pointless and a little crazy) and in Christian circles (because God isn't someone we can or should seek to manipulate with our vows). Infertility, however, has challenged my understanding of prayer in uncomfortable but ultimately healing ways. Until the grief of barrenness visited my life, I never noticed how profoundly bargaining has shaped some of the most time-honored and transformative prayers of our tradition—many of them uttered by barren women against all reasonable hope. I never noticed how bold and brave (and almost scandalously *persistent*) these women were.

Rather than defining or analyzing prayer, in this chapter I offer a series of reflections, each of which loosely addresses the difficult questions infertility has raised within me when it comes to God and prayer. How long (and how hard) should one pray for children—or anything else, for that matter? What is prayer, particularly when we are angry, confused, or desperate? And, as long as we are being honest: why bother with prayer at all?

∞

"People have told me 'God knows what He is doing,' and 'It probably means parenthood just isn't right for you, so just accept that.' It's so hurtful I have stopped talking to the friends and family members who say these things."
—*Adrienne*

∞

"AND ANNA PUT OFF HER GARMENTS OF MOURNING"

The scene on which this chapter is based immediately follows Anna's altercation with Judith. After the latter's stinging words, Anna retreats to the garden—under the laurel tree. But first, she washes her face and dons her wedding dress (I'm guessing it was a bit tattered, having spent the last half-century in storage). Why the costume change—has Anna finally moved beyond her grief? Has God, as the Psalmist once wrote, "taken off [her] sackcloth / and clothed [her] with joy"? (Psalm 30:11, NRSV). Hardly. Anna has more or less had it—she's done pretending.

In shedding her mourning clothes, Anna relinquishes the artificial script of widowhood she's been clinging to—she knows Joachim isn't dead. Maybe she knew all along he was still alive; the "widowhood" phase was little more than a slightly less awkward guise for the real issue: barrenness. And now, with the biological deck stacked against her, with her husband facing his own demons in the wilderness, she gets down to business with God. Why the wedding dress? Because, in a strange way, it's the only thing she has left to bargain with.

In the Old Testament, wedding clothing symbolized righteousness, a kind of exculpatory covering. The Prophet Isaiah, for example, likens the "garments of salvation" to wedding accessories:

> I will greatly rejoice in the Lord,
> my whole being shall exult in my God;
> for he has clothed me with the garments of salvation,
> he has covered me with the robe of righteousness,
> as a bridegroom decks himself with a garland,
> and as a bride adorns herself with her jewels. (Is 61:10, NRSV)

In the New Testament, of course, bridal symbolism is bound up with the Church, weddings and wedding banquets with the eschatological union of Christ (the Bridegroom) with His bride: "And I saw the holy city, the new Jerusalem, coming down out of heaven from God, prepared as a bride adorned for her husband" (Rev 21:2, NRSV).

On one level, then, Anna's choice of clothing anticipates the transfiguration of humanity into the bride of Christ, the Church. The symbolism in this chapter of the *Protoevangelium* is so ripe it's practically falling off the (laurel?) tree. (And speaking of trees, we're in a *garden*. Gardens being places of life and fruit, the setting only highlights Anna's barrenness and the anguish that has resulted from it. It also ties her prayers to the Garden of Eden—where humanity once fell into sin—and the Garden of Gethsemane, where Christ will accept the cup of suffering placed before Him and enact the restoration of our former status before God.)

But we still haven't really identified all of what's going on with this wedding dress. To do that, we need to remember a second, related line of symbolism at work in the biblical imagination. Throughout Scripture, brides and bridal garments also recalled original innocence or fidelity to God. In Jeremiah, for example, the Lord recalls Israel's faithfulness in the desert:

I remember the devotion of your youth,
your love as a bride,
how you followed me in the wilderness,
in a land not sown. (Jer. 2:2, NRSV)

As much as Israel relied on God during their years of wandering in
the *barren* desert (a rather forgiving recollection, if you ask me), by
Jeremiah's time, they had strayed from God and forgotten His goodness. Later in the same chapter, the Lord admonishes Israel for their
inattention, driving His grief home with yet another bridal analogy:

Have I been a wilderness to Israel,
or a land of thick darkness?
Why then do my people say, "We are free,
we will come to you no more"?
Can a girl forget her ornaments,
or a bride her attire?
Yet my people have forgotten me,
days without number. (Jer. 2:31–32, NRSV)

Just as it would be unfathomable for a woman to forget what she
wore on her wedding day, so it is unthinkable that Israel could forget
God or the time He nourished them in the desert—yet they had.

I have been remembering the above verses as I pore over this
episode of Anna's plight, because in many ways her chosen attire
is almost a response to God's continuous call to Israel through the
prophets. Just as God calls His people to remember their wedding
garments, Anna flips the script and asks the same of God. *Don't you
remember my wedding day, when I entered into this union with my husband full of hope and faithfulness?* her wardrobe decision seems to cry
to Him. *Have you forgotten how trustingly I followed You into this desert of barrenness?*

It's a lament so many of us can relate to, particularly if we were

married in an Orthodox service, which stresses God's blessing
through childbearing over a dozen times in a scant hour and a half.
How many of us have looked at our wedding pictures and not wondered, "What about those prayers, God? What were they for if not
for children? Have You forgotten us?" Of course, perhaps Anna
wears her wedding garments to challenge *herself*—to remind herself
of her former way of being, to recover all those innocent hopes that
had frayed over the years. But I read it much more as a challenge to
God, daring Him to look upon Anna and finally remember her, her
marriage, her devotion.

And that, to me, is bold. It's hitting the ball of barrenness back
to God's side of the court. It may look a little arrogant, but in truth
it's the opposite. It's taking God at His word. It's respecting God
enough to treat Him like God, not some idol to be touched with
soft gloves lest it disintegrate or lash out. It's holding nothing back,
throwing one's entire being at the mercy of a God who said He would
be faithful.

"*In general, infertility has changed my relationship to
prayer for the worse. There are many times when I am angry
and just cannot pray.*" —Nadia

PRAY AND (DON'T?) MAKE YOUR VOWS
BEFORE THE LORD

Judging by this scene, I am guessing Anna did not have the same
Sunday school teacher I grew up with. Aside from the fact she lived
two millennia before I was born, my teacher taught me something

when I was about five that Anna appears not to have learned. And that is: never bargain with God. The specific phrasing was, never make "if-then" statements to God (e.g. "*If* you grant me this request, *then* I will be nicer to people"). My teacher explained we should not be too demanding of God—it's prideful.

I remember her instruction so clearly because at the time, I was a compulsive bargainer. Back then, my mother was pregnant with my second sibling, and I had already been brokering some covert deals with God to ensure the baby in her belly would turn out to be a sister (the one brother I already had was quite enough, I told Him). Either my Sunday school teacher was right, or I stopped bargaining prematurely at her insistence, because I now have two brothers.

As humorously as this episode now strikes me, I internalized her teaching in ways I never fully realized until infertility entered my life. By then, the "no if-then statements" sentiment had expanded into an entire, subconscious rule of prayer that centered on docile passivity and blind acceptance. It's better to be polite and restrained with God, I reasoned, than prideful and manipulative—or worse: angry, inconsolable, or desperate.

This ethos got me through some truly horrific situations and, honestly, probably prolonged a few abusive relationships. But it couldn't stand up to infertility (which says a lot about how deep the grief of childlessness runs). For the first time in my life, I didn't think I could just accept the cup God had placed before me. At times, I have found myself desperate, resentful, and ridiculously fearful about the prospect of lifelong childlessness. But for a long time, I didn't have any other tools, any other picture in my mind of what prayer and faithfulness to God were supposed to look like.

Until I found Hannah, or rather saw her through new eyes and promptly wondered where she'd been all my life.

"I have long felt hesitant about praying for myself or making specific requests of God, even for other people. How do I know what is good for me? This inclination is, in fact, one of the things that has attracted me to the patterns of prayer that I find in Orthodoxy: praying the Jesus Prayer for myself and others and trusting that God's mercy and wisdom abundantly suffice for all our needs. But in recent months I've started making requests that we be granted a child if it be God's will. I do not quite understand why, but I think that if we are unable to have children, it will give me more of a sense of purpose: that door was closed for a reason." —Brianna

HANNAH: A LESSON IN BARGAINING

The biblical figure that Anna—and her prayer—most resembles is her namesake, Hannah.[44] Although Hannah would become the mother of Samuel, we first meet her as the barren wife of Elkanah (1 Sam. 1:2—2:21): "He had two wives; the name of the one was Hannah, and the name of the other Peninnah. Peninnah had children, but Hannah had no children." This setup echoes the "it's complicated" relationship of sisters Rebekah and Leah (Rebekah being the primary but barren wife of Jacob, Leah his fertile but less-loved wife). Hannah's childlessness also hearkens back to Sarah, the most memorable barren matriarch of the Old Testament. Despite these similarities, though, Hannah is different from her predecessors:

Hannah, unlike Sarah and Rebekah, never doubts her capacity for motherhood. Although vexed by Peninnah, Hannah does not enter into the rivalry that characterizes the matriarchal narratives. With a loving (but tactless) husband and a jealous rival wife, Hannah keeps her counsel and her suffering to herself.[45]

This assessment holds true. Despite endless taunts from Peninnah and a sympathetic but ultimately clueless husband, Hannah reserved the sharp edge of her grief for God alone. Year after year, she poured out her request for a child to Him. In his sermons on this passage, St. John Chrysostom repeatedly marvels at just how *long* Hannah remained faithful in prayer: "not two or three days, not twenty or a hundred, not a thousand or twice as much; instead . . . for many years the woman was grieving and distressed. . . . Yet she showed no impatience, nor did the length of time undermine her values."[46]

Hannah managed to walk that fine line between hope—evidenced by her ongoing prayers—and reality. She didn't let despair "undermine her values," as St. John points out, or rob her of her love for God. But that doesn't mean it was easy. Between Peninnah's taunts, Elkanah's broken efforts to help, and the unrelenting barrenness, Hannah eventually became so distressed that she stopped eating. So fervent were her silent prayers that Eli, the priest observing her at the temple, assumed she was drunk. Hannah rebuffed him: "No, my lord, I am a woman deeply troubled; I have drunk neither wine nor strong drink, but I have been pouring out my soul before the Lord. Do not regard your servant as a worthless woman, for I have been speaking out of my great anxiety and vexation all this time" (1 Sam 1:15–16, NRSV).

Before she left the temple, she promised God that if He would only open her womb (she specifically requested a male child), she would raise him as a Nazirite, one consecrated to the Lord. With that, as St. John Chrysostom so memorably puts it, "as though softened by the flood of tears and warmed with the pangs, the womb began to stir in that wonderful fertility."[47] Out of her tears and long-suffering supplications, she became pregnant with the Prophet Samuel.

It's a beautiful story in theory, but in practice, it's another one of those tales we don't quite know what to do with nowadays. By the time God hears her prayers, Hannah is basically a mess: crying, starving, barely coherent, bearing the appearance of a drunk. The God *I* know does not stand for that kind of thing—prim and proper, that's how I was taught to pray. And another thing: Hannah doesn't just pray. She full on, *explicitly* bargains with God: *if* you give me a ~~child at all~~ son, *then* I will do something for You in return. And the most audacious part of the whole narrative is that, far from turning Hannah away, God fulfills her request—right down to the desired gender of the child. Once again, this is not the God that I know. Which makes me wonder just who this God is that I supposedly know so well.

To be honest, I'm not entirely sure what the lesson for infertile people like me is in all of this. I suppose the easy answer is that God responded to Hannah's boldness because of the reverence, faith, and humility that underscored her request, which only He could fully discern. Still, cultivating those virtues is a lifelong process, and I think Hannah's (and Anna's) prayers have something more immediate to tell us that perhaps we have forgotten: they remind us, perhaps when few others in our lives will, that it's okay (even laudable) to keep asking God for the same thing over and over, year after year, month after month. I think we need to be reminded that God can handle more of us (and our desperation) than we think; that for all the times we've been overly cautious and polite in prayer, perhaps it's time we err on the side of being a mess, of making deals and bargains, if that's what prompts us to cry out to God and for once in our fleeting lives be absolutely real before Him. No, this may not ensure

He will answer our prayers according to our exact specifications, but we already know that. And deep down, we also know that having a baby is ultimately less important than the assurance that God has not forsaken us, that goodness and mercy shall follow us, that futility won't have the last word. Things may not turn out the way we pray, but that doesn't mean God is ashamed of us for asking (and asking some more).

Disclaimer: I've never bargained with God for a child, at least not in the way Hannah did. Every time I picture myself in her shoes, my palms start sweating. Deep down, this is probably because I lack the faith she had. I don't have the courage to lock myself into that kind of ultimatum with God. Assuming He *were* to comply, which is a big *if* (Lord, help my unbelief), am I really willing to give anything in return? After all, Hannah didn't just demand, she offered. She expressed her willingness to raise her son in an unusual, above-and-beyond way that required caution and sacrifices for both her and her petitioned-for child. If I'm honest, sometimes I just want a kid, no strings (or Nazirite vows, or risks, or adoption protocols) attached. Hannah's story is like a mirror, revealing my latent sense of entitlement and faithlessness. Of course, I'm working on this. But what I've learned so far is that, contrary to my well-intentioned Sunday school teacher, it usually takes more humility than pride to truly, sincerely make demands of God.

In the midst of my journey, I am helped by an observation St. John Chrysostom made in his second homily on the story of Hannah. Reflecting on her long-lasting barrenness, he said:

> It was nature that was out of sorts, requiring intervention from on high—hence she . . . had recourse to the Lord of nature, nor did she desist until she had persuaded him to cancel her childlessness, open her womb, and make the sterile woman a mother. Blessed is she, therefore, even on this account, not for being a mother, but

for becoming one after not being one: while the former is a common attribute of nature, the latter was this woman's commendable achievement.[48]

For Hannah, prayer wasn't just a form of therapy to help her learn to passively accept God's will. She refused to stop pleading with God until nature was back in alignment, and she was fully willing to uphold her end of the bargain. In doing so, she rose above the laws of nature. For her, conception became a miraculous achievement, and it was *her* achievement—not her husband's, and not even strictly God's. This is a startling icon of prayer, and womanhood, that we would do well to visit and revisit often in our journey through infertility and beyond.

"In the years of this struggle I have done my share of crying, reading the Psalms, and hugging my husband. This cross, first with infertility and now with recurrent miscarriage, is quite a lonely one on this Earth. And yet in my more faithful moments, it also feels like a special calling. I have received so many blessings and so much strength over the years, that I can honestly say that, with God's help, I'm actually not angry, not resentful of God or jealous of anyone else. As God has "become greater," and I "have become less," I feel great joy when I hear that my friends are pregnant again, and I feel their pain when the demands of their large families and closely spaced children overwhelm them."
—Teresa

"I THINK WE SHOULD FIGHT"

As I consider the legacy of prayer Hannah and Anna have given us, I can't help but remember an episode of my favorite television show, *The Office*.[49] It centers on Jim and Pam, whose relationship blossomed over the first handful of seasons of the show, but who now face a rough patch in their marriage. Despite their best efforts, a separation seems imminent. In this episode, right in the middle of all the tension, they realize it's Valentine's Day. Although tempted to blow off the holiday given the state of their marriage, Jim and Pam remember they have scheduled a double lunch date long in advance with another couple they know, Brian and Alyssa. Reluctantly, they head to the restaurant, but only Brian is there to meet them. It turns out that he and Alyssa have recently separated.

In shock, Jim wonders aloud what happened—they seemed so close. He tries to reassure Brian by reminding him that every couple has arguments.

"That's the thing," Brian explained. "When we were fighting, it weirdly felt like the relationship was still alive. And it wasn't until we stopped fighting that we realized that it was over."

Later in the episode, Jim is about to leave for his other job in another city. He wasn't planning on leaving until the next day, but since he and Pam still haven't managed to resolve anything, he decides it's best to leave early. As viewers, we understand he's giving up not only on Valentine's Day, but on the marriage as a whole—this is their last chance to work things out. Of course, this being Hollywood, Pam stops him at the last possible moment.

"I think you should stay," she tells him, an uncharacteristically assertive tone in her voice.

"I feel like we're just going to fight," Jim says. "You really want to fight on Valentine's Day?"

But Pam is adamant. With tears in her eyes, she replies, "I don't think you should go to Philly tonight. I think that you should stay and I think we should fight."

So he does stay, and they do fight, and eventually, over the course of a few tumultuous episodes, their marriage is restored.

Sometimes our relationship with God is not unlike Jim and Pam's marriage. So often, we encounter things about God and His actions (or seeming lack thereof) that make us angry, sad, or completely confused. That's not the problem; that's just a relationship being a relationship. The real trouble begins when we stop fighting with Him, that is, when we stop coming to Him with our cares or frustrations or questions—trivial and repetitive though they may seem; stop expecting anything of Him, stop putting any of our deep, interior selves on the line before Him. Eventually we wake up and realize we just don't *love* Him anymore. That is, we don't love how dead and repressed we've become whenever we're around Him. So we leave.

For a while, I tried accepting childlessness as God's will for my life—it seemed like the holy thing to do. It's not that I ceased praying altogether, I just limited myself to the safe things, the topics I knew God and I already agreed on—prayers for the poor and the hungry, for captives and their salvation, and for summer in Canada to last more than a measly month or two. One day I realized I hadn't accepted anything, I'd just locked my deepest self in a box every time I came to God. Somehow in the process, I managed to accumulate a hard crust of resentment toward Him that I am still working to till.

Some people do accept their childlessness, voluntarily—they learn to live with it, they give thanks and move on. That's okay, but now I know that's not me. I don't accept childlessness as God's one and only will for my life, or rather I don't accept the *acceptance* of my childlessness as God's will. I will have to move on from my childlessness eventually—nature will see to that one way or the other. But in the meantime, I plan to carry on throwing my whole self at this thing, and at God Himself: prayer, hope, tears, more prayers, sometimes anger, often love. Because even if I never have biological children, I want to remember this season as a time of being fully alive, of unpacking my pain rather than boxing it up. And because I would rather be a mess with God than be artificially and passive-aggressively calm apart from Him.

But most of all, because sometimes, instead of walking out on Him, we just need to stay. And we need to fight.

"Honestly, I don't want to pray. I tend towards feeling angry at God. To keep me praying, my prayers have been reduced to a daily request in front of the icon of Christ (at the advice of my spiritual father) to, 'Help me today to be able to feel that you love me.'" —Emilia

WHEN PRAYER ISN'T POLITE

The prayers of Anna and Hannah are not outliers. They come out of a long tradition of arguing with God, a tradition that is also evident in the way people interacted with Christ. The furtive (and achingly repetitive) cries of the Psalms, the persistent prayers of Moses, Job, and countless prophets; the faith of the Canaanite woman, Zacchaeus, and so many others who cut holes in houses, climbed trees, stalked, nagged, whined, pressed in against, and compulsively touched Christ for healing—they all shared a common, if off-putting, trait: they couldn't take no for an answer. Of course, we lump this quality under the more spiritually acceptable guises of "persistence" and "perseverance," but come on, they were stubborn. And annoying. And, frankly, I wouldn't have blamed God for taking out a restraining order on some of them.

Of course, some of this is cultural—I've been married to a Greek long enough to know that what passes for "politeness" differs greatly depending on how close to the Mediterranean one finds oneself. I'll never forget when my mother-in-law suddenly stood up at our wedding reception and began yelling at the top of her lungs in Greek. The level of intensity in her voice made the hair on the back of my neck stand up. "What's going on? What's she upset about?" I asked my husband, assuming the lamb must have run out or something. "She's praying for us. She's giving us her blessing," he whispered incredulously. "This is an important moment." Sure enough, as I looked around, our Greek guests were smiling and nodding, some of them dabbing tears from the corners of their eyes. My American friends, on the other hand, were all but ducking for cover.

Still, cultural norms don't *fully* account for the brazen, pushy tone that so often accompanies prayers or petitions made in the Bible. What does God do when Job (whose friends have even grown tired of his prayers) once again demands God show His face? He shows Himself. What does Christ say when the Canaanite woman refuses to be sent away (Matt. 15:21–28)? He applauds her "great faith" and promptly heals her daughter. Of course, God doesn't always answer people's requests in the way they expect, but the Old and New Testaments alike affirm tenacity and stubbornness in prayer more often than not.

I have been collecting stories from the Bible that involve people being bold before God, saving them up for rainy days when I am tempted to cower into apathy and despondency toward Him. One of those rainy days came when a faithful Orthodox, seminary-trained friend warned me not to pray too long or too hard to get pregnant.

"I knew a couple who did that," she calmly explained. "God finally answered their prayer, but the baby had Down syndrome. Just be careful what you wish for."

It's been several years since she told me that, and I still don't know what she was trying to say. Does she believe the Down syndrome was a punishment—and for prayer? I don't know. What I do know is that infertility brings out some of our worst and most fearful attitudes towards God. I hope we would never tell someone who is unemployed, or has a wayward son or a mother with Alzheimer's, to just accept their distress as God's will. We would never caution someone with cancer against praying too much. Not even when the cancer returns, nor when it metastasizes ten years later. Not even when every medical professional has given a terminal diagnosis. Of course, we might recognize how unlikely a recovery would be, and we might pray for a death that is ultimately "painless and blameless." But, deep down, part of us would still keep praying for a miracle until the last breath.

But infertility, I guess, is different. Maybe that's because, like leprosy or plagues of locusts, it's biblical. Because of this, it gets mixed up with moral judgment to a degree other ailments don't. It's also tied to gender norms in ways other medical conditions aren't. When you add all this up, at first glance it may seem more pious in a way for infertile women to accept barrenness as their God-given fate. I say "women," here, because men (at least those I've spoken or corresponded with) are less likely to be steered toward acceptance. Why? My guess is because in our current culture, passivity and compliance are traditionally deemed feminine rather than masculine qualities. Men are the warriors, the breadwinners, the side of the equation that fights and wrestles and goes for it. Women are to take what they're given—quietly, sweetly, and ideally with smiles on our faces. This is, of course, a gross generalization, but I know few women (and men) today who feel they fully live up to the unspoken gender ideals our culture so often enforces.

Perhaps that's why I find figures like Hannah, Anna, and Joachim (not to mention pretty much everyone else in the Bible) so refreshingly perplexing. They remind me that faith isn't about being masculine or feminine as our society dictates; it's about being godly. And godliness is both messy and simple, it's courageous and meek, it's patient and persistent, it's personal and communal—it's all the paradoxes.

WHERE IS DESPAIR?

What role does despair play in Anna and Joachim's story? You may recall that despair (often termed depression) was the penultimate stage of grief according to Elisabeth Kübler-Ross. For her, depression results from finally facing the reality of one's inevitable or unchangeable circumstances and is therefore a necessary precursor to acceptance. It is characterized by thoughts like "I can't change the situation, so why bother?" or "I will probably never have children, so why care about the future?" Explaining Kübler-Ross's concept of despair, Christine Gregory writes:

> Depression . . . represents the emptiness we feel when we are living in reality and realize the person or situation is gone or over. In this stage, you might withdraw from life, feel numb, live in a fog, and not want to get out of bed. The world might seem too much and too overwhelming for you to face. You don't want to be around others, don't feel like talking, and experience feelings of hopelessness.[50]

While certain symptoms of despair seem present with Anna in the garden—withdrawal, for example, and deep sadness—I find it difficult to categorize the scene as true "depression." For one thing, she *hasn't* accepted her circumstances. As forlorn as she becomes, she never gives up on the possibility that her circumstances might be changed for the better. Her despair is tinged with just enough hope and tenacity that she never fully turns her back on God.

Even her withdrawal from human company doesn't seem like the kind of isolation ordinarily associated with "complicated grief," our contemporary term for grief that has become debilitating, unnecessarily prolonged, or otherwise concerning. Sometimes you just need to be alone, which is to say, with God. Even Christ stepped back from the crowds, and even He wept, prayed fervently, and experienced distress to the extreme that it manifested itself physically (as when He sweat blood in the Garden of Gethsemane).

Anna's intense sorrow is an image of despair that serves us well in our own grief. It recalls the words of the Psalmist, who proclaimed that even "If I should descend into Hades, You would be there" (Ps. 138/139:8). I am reminded of the saying often attributed to St. Silouan: "Keep your mind in hell, and despair not." Although this quote is frequently cited as a practice to aid repentance—in that we must never allow our pride to soar too far above our own need for salvation—it offers wisdom to the grieving process as well, particularly those moments or seasons marked first and foremost by the kind of anguish that has no words. In deep grief, seemingly no effort is required to keep one's mind in hell. Indeed, the sadness and darkness of our circumstances may press in on all sides until they become a hell in and of themselves. And yet, it is possible to be fully immersed in grief—to be facing the deep lacerations of one's existence—without giving up. When in hell, when beneath the laurel tree of anguish, when empty, when seemingly abandoned: despair not.

KEEPING WATCH FOR HOPE

Around the same time I was first told to "just accept" infertility as God's will, one of my best friends (who got married nearly a year after I did) got pregnant with baby #1. We knew how difficult it would be to continue our closeness—not just because of the logistical challenges a little one presents to ordinary adult relationships, but because of the glaring emotional tension between her pregnancy and my infertility.

"How can I be a good friend?" she asked me once, as we entered into this new season together.

"I need you to keep hoping for me," I told her, the words coming out of my mouth before I had a chance to consider them.

I didn't know then exactly what I meant, but the more we have returned to the conversation, the more I have learned the truth behind my words. I didn't need her sympathy or advice, nor did I need her to encourage *me* to have hope. I needed her to stand with me in the tension field that is hope, to bear that burden with me, especially on days I myself didn't feel particularly hopeful. I think people start pulling out acceptance when they sense that I am sad and have been sad for a long time—they imagine that maybe it would all be easier if I just let it go and gave up.

"But that's not actually how it works," I explained to my friend. "It helps to know that there is at least one woman on this planet with whom I can be sad about this, even for long stretches, without her rushing in to alleviate the tension by giving up hope altogether. So I hereby give you permission to be hopeful for me, to hope against hope, to pray against the odds for me."

As I saw it then, my request was not unlike Christ asking His disciples to sit watch with Him in the Garden (which perhaps reveals a bit of my ~~pride~~ flair for melodrama). But instead of keeping watch for my cross, I needed someone to help me keep vigil for hope. It's a long, difficult wait either way. But alone, without a friend to help bear the burden of hope, I knew I'd fall asleep to the fullness of what God has set before me.

It's been several years since that conversation, and my friend has continued to hope with me—gently, inconspicuously, but enough that it has helped me hold space for goodness and expectation. They say you can't drive a parked car. And to hope, for me, is to drive the car—or at least keep it in neutral. It keeps me moving. It keeps the conversation of prayer going through all the stages of grief. God can (and, believe me, does) steer that car wherever He wants, but if I stop hoping, I will coast to a standstill. I will, as Fr. Geoffrey put it, stop winding the reel of faith—the inertia of grief will hijack the story before I learn to see beyond the despair and sadness.

And in all the hoping and relinquishing, despairing and praying, I am learning something new under the laurel tree: *Alas! To what have I been likened?* Anna once lamented when she stood in a place similar to ours. And the plain truth is, she wasn't and would never be like any other creature—not because of her barrenness, but because of her faith, her willingness to pray (and keep praying) to God in that paradoxical union of despair and expectation. That kind of faith, I'd imagine, is a lonely labor, but show me anything else that is worth striving for. I'll wait.

DISCUSSION AND REFLECTION QUESTIONS

1. What is bargaining? As a stage of grief? As a form of prayer?

2. What is something you've been taught about prayer that has turned out to be untrue or inconsistent with understandings of prayer in the Bible or the Church?

3. How has infertility challenged your experience of prayer for the better? For worse?

4. What challenges you about Anna's prayer beneath the laurel tree? What about Hannah's prayer for Samuel? What other examples from Scripture or Tradition inspire you when it comes to prayer and faith?

5. What is the value of fighting or arguing with God? Should we place limits or parameters on this out of humility?

CHAPTER 8

Thanksgiving

And, behold, an angel of the Lord stood by, saying: Anna, Anna, the Lord has heard your prayer, and you shall conceive, and shall bring forth; and your seed shall be spoken of in all the world. And Anna said: As the Lord my God lives, if I beget either male or female, I will bring it as a gift to the Lord my God; and it shall minister to Him in holy things all the days of its life.

And, behold, two angels came, saying to her: Behold, Joachim your husband is coming with his flocks. For an angel of the Lord went down to him, saying: Joachim, Joachim, the Lord God has heard your prayer. Go down hence; for, behold, your wife Anna shall conceive. And Joachim went down and called his shepherds, saying: Bring me hither ten she-lambs without spot or blemish, and they shall be for the Lord my God; and bring me twelve tender calves, and they shall be for the priests and the elders; and a hundred goats for all the people. And, behold, Joachim came with his flocks; and Anna stood by the gate, and saw Joachim coming, and she ran and hung upon his neck, saying: Now I know that the Lord God has blessed

*me exceedingly; for, behold the widow no longer a widow, and
I the childless shall conceive. And Joachim rested the first day
in his house.*

PROTOEVANGELIUM OF JAMES, 4

My husband and I recently became an uncle and an aunt for the first time. I will never forget when my brother announced that he and my sister-in-law were expecting: I was at the grocery store, trying to figure out how to avoid dropping a bulk package of toilet paper while answering my phone. As soon as I heard the words, I definitely lost my grip on the toilet paper, along with my composure—they had been trying to conceive nearly twice as long as we had, and for all intents and purposes had given up.

Despite my happiness, I couldn't quite get on board with the relief everyone else seemed to feel—not because of jealousy or envy, but fear. Pregnancies are precarious. They say an opera isn't over until the fat lady sings, and for me, infertility isn't over until a baby cries. I waited for the hammer to fall as my sister-in-law progressed through each trimester, but it never did. It wasn't until months and months later, when their tiny son took his first breaths, that I felt the cloud of their childlessness had really been parted. Only then did I feel I could truly give thanks to God for this gift of a nephew.

It is human nature to postpone gratitude until after the fact—after we receive what we've prayed for, after our dreams come true, after we can see, taste, smell, or touch whatever it is we've been holding out for. Even when we get an inkling of what's to come, to protect ourselves from the pain of disillusionment, we wait until it comes to pass before opening our hearts to thanksgiving and to God.

Joachim and Anna rose above this ordinary human tendency and gave thanks before they conceived—indeed, before they had even Done the Deed. Yes, they had the advantage of angels foretelling their miraculous conception, but this doesn't always translate to thanksgiving—Sarah from the Old Testament, and Zechariah from the New, both reacted less than graciously when an angel heralded their good fortune. Anticipating the conception of Mary, Anna and Joachim offered their personal thanks to God before reuniting.

The true "good news," here, was not simply that they would soon be with child, but that salvation was on its way in a more global sense (*"your seed shall be spoken of in all the world"*). Thus, their glad tidings are our glad tidings, whether we come to bear children or not. Likewise, their response of thanksgiving is the eucharistic life we are all called to, regardless of whether our prayers for children are granted. In her famous five stages of grief, Elizabeth Kübler-Ross points to acceptance as the ideal destination of grief. The purpose of acceptance is for a person to acknowledge that although what is happening to them is sad, they will ultimately be okay. They may not be cured, life may not go back to normal, yet in a broader existential sense, "all will be well," to quote Julian of Norwich. But as monumental as acceptance can be, Christian witness calls us to ascend beyond it to gratitude.

This chapter reflects on thanksgiving from a variety of angles, integrating it into the experience of infertility for couples and individuals. The kind of thanksgiving I envision runs deeper than the trite advice we may receive from well-meaning loved ones to "just be thankful" for what we have, regardless of our lack of children. The Bible doesn't actually command us to *be* thankful, but to *give* thanks—to God, in all circumstances (1 Thess. 5:18). This isn't a feeling but an action. It is not a means of forgetting or masking our pain but learning to truly dwell and act within the full spectrum of the pain and joy granted to us in this life. Thanksgiving is about gathering ourselves from the scattered corners of our sorrow and presenting our whole being in thank offering to our Creator. As we do so, thanksgiving enables us to reclaim our God-given freedom in the face of struggles that can seem outside our control and God's providence.

"Since beginning to struggle with infertility, I have become more thankful for godchildren, for nephews and nieces, and for the time that I have with my husband." —Adrienne

HOW (NOT) TO RESPOND

If an angel ever appears in your old age and announces you will bear a child contrary to any and all laws of nature, here are some ways you *could* respond. You could scoff, as Sarah did. You could yell "It's about time!" You could grab the baby and run away before God has a chance to change His mind. You could repeat the news loudly enough for your petty maidservant to hear ("Did you get that, Judith? Turns out I'm not so cursed after all!").

Here's how you probably *wouldn't* respond: immediately vow to give the baby away, out of gratitude, no questions asked. Which, of course, is exactly what Anna does. In making her pledge, Anna effectively signs over her parental rights to the temple (later in the *Protoevangelium*, Joachim and Anna will present a weaned, toddling Theotokos to God, whereupon they basically exit the story). Raising the bar even higher, Anna places no conditions on her offering—unlike her Old Testament namesake, Hannah, she doesn't request the child be a specific gender. Whether it is a boy or girl, Anna vows to offer it in service of the living God.

Really, Anna? I mean, wouldn't your husband's beyond-excessive livestock offering suffice? Wasn't having a baby the whole point? What unsettles me most about Anna's vow is not merely that she offers her precious child back to God, but that she does so immediately, instinctively, as though that had been the plan all along.

And maybe it was. Maybe the anguish and prayers of Anna and Joachim were never really about a baby as such. Perhaps they were never asking for a feast, just a morsel of God's mercy, a sign of His favor, a chance to hold this child in their arms for a scant few moments, to taste and see the Lord is good before departing from this earth. This was not about parenthood for parenthood's sake, but about synergy—the joy of being made worthy of cooperating with God.

And that is a scary thing to spend your life longing for. In some ways, hope for a baby is easier to bear than what we're truly after: assurance that we haven't been forgotten, cast aside, overlooked, deemed inadequate, faulty, unworthy. We want to know—with our senses, our bodies—that this God we've been trying to serve all these years is who He says He is: a God of mercy and compassion. We want to be sure He sees us, knows us, loves us. And we want this certainty, too, from our spouses. Will they remain by our side if our bodies cannot do this most basic thing?

There have been times when this assurance comes naturally, if unexpectedly—moments when infertility has allowed me to see my soul as a ship unmoored to this world by children or biology, carried out onto the churning sea of faith, "the reckless, raging fury that they call the love of God," as Christian songwriter Rich Mullins once sang.[51] Somehow all the waves of grief have made plain how unconditionally loved I am—by the God who made me, by my husband who united with me. Does our childlessness deepen the quality of our love, since we have no one to tie us to one another, nothing to offer God or one another, procreatively speaking? I don't know. But in those brief moments, it has seemed—beyond my human comprehension—that all this barrenness is some kind of tremendous gift for the awareness it affords me.

Still, there are many, many more times when I just want the baby—I grow impatient in all the waiting and praying and wondering. Synergy, evidently, is a learning process. God's helping me work on it.

"In retrospect, infertility was the first thing in my life that I could not conquer by working harder, spending more money, or studying more. It was like hitting a brick wall. It was incredibly painful, but it did bring me closer to God. Now I am thankful for it." —Kristen

AN ICON OF RECONCILIATION

Countless times, I've experienced the irritating serendipity of doing or saying the same thing as my husband right when we are in the middle of a disagreement. It could be as simple as sending the same text message at the same time, walking out of the house wearing the same color shirt, or being the only people in church who laugh at a subtle joke in a priest's sermon. Just when some perceived transgression has driven me to my high horse, I see myself in my husband and realize how intertwined our hearts are—despite (or because of) ourselves.

This scene in Joachim and Anna's story makes me think of moments like this. Across the chasm of grief and separation, they both react the same way to the angels' good news: they give thanks.

Immediately. Abundantly. Without knowing what the other is doing. First Anna dedicates their child-yet-to-be-conceived to the temple; then Joachim sets aside a frankly obscene quantity of lambs, calves, and goats to offer to God. They don't wait to ask each other's permission, they don't waste time wondering and searching for what to give God; they offer up what is at once most immediate and most precious to them. By the time they come back together, no explanation is needed. They are, most endearingly, on the same page.

All this bespeaks a profound faith, not only in God, but also in one another and in their marriage. Their thanksgiving forms the basis of their reconciliation as a couple, a reminder that giving thanks evokes our truest and most authentic selves. While the sharp edges of grief can harden and isolate us, thanksgiving softens and opens us—to ourselves, to others, to God, to hope. In a sense, Joachim and Anna must return to themselves before returning to one another.

The moment of their reconciliation is rendered beautifully (and more than a little suggestively) in the icon of the Conception of the Theotokos. In the foreground, Joachim and Anna are locked in a tender embrace, staring into one another's eyes. In some versions of the icon, they are standing beneath the sparse laurel tree where Anna has just been praying; other times they appear in front of the city walls of Jerusalem, marking Joachim's return to the land of the living from the barren wilderness. And for anyone who still isn't clear on where this embrace is heading, a bed is often visible just behind them (positioned in front of the royal gates of Jerusalem, prefiguring Mary the Theotokos, the "royal gates" through whom Christ will enter the world). The icon takes pains to emphasize that this will be an "ordinary" act of procreation:

> Without being explicit, it is boldly confessed that, whilst a miracle granted to a barren couple, the conception of St. Mary happened through natural means. This can be compared with Icons of

the Annunciation, which could be described as the Conception of Jesus Christ: in those icons Mary is not shown with Joseph; Mary remained a virgin.[52]

But for all the theological clues found in this icon, what really affects me is the embrace—specifically the eye contact. It is, in a word, intense. Joachim and Anna aren't just looking fondly at each other; they are boring into one another's retinas, and it's a little awkward. Their gaze is more than a visual euphemism for other forms of intimacy. It's almost as though Joachim and Anna, man and woman, are seeing one another truly for the first time in all of human history. This is husband and wife restored to their mutual status of helpmates, co-laborers in the same Garden, simultaneously comprehending all that men and women lost in the Fall and all that we regain when we (re)unite ourselves with one another in the fear of God.

As joyous and penetrating as this moment is, the same icon bears witness to the turmoil of the couple's childlessness. In some versions of the icon, Joachim and Anna are also visible in vignette form in the upper corners, in somber prayer but at an obvious distance from one another. Thus, the icon gathers all the frames of their experience—the frames of grief and the frame of joy—into one story. Echoing Fr. Geoffrey's analogy I mentioned in the introduction of this book, it's a visible expression of the full reel of faith. Without Joachim and Anna's grief, we would not appreciate the magnitude of their reconciliation. And without their thanksgiving, we would stagnate in their sorrow—and our own.

"Looking back, I am grateful we did not have children. It meant I was able to give up my job to become my father-in-law's full-time caregiver. He lived with us for his last eight

years of his life, and became Orthodox three years before his repose." —Lorna

WHEN NATURE BECOMES MIRACLE

For those of us dealing with infertility, a major impediment to thanksgiving is the assumption that children are supposed to come automatically, a universal law of biology written into the code of creation. The inability to fulfill this basic process feels not just *un*natural, but almost unconstitutional—wasn't the right to bear children in there somewhere, along with the rights to bear arms and speak freely?

Not exactly, as most of us reading this have learned the hard way. Perhaps the paradoxically most difficult and beautiful thing infertility imparts to us (and to the world) is that nature—even the most given and taken-for-granted aspects of it—is miracle, and miracle is not ours to maneuver. This idea is expanded on in a poignant reflection by the somewhat controversial Jewish rabbi, Shmuel Boteach, called "When Nature Becomes Miracle." He begins:

> When we observe a consistent pattern we call it nature. And what does nature do to us? It conceals God's involvement with the world. When we see that which God repeats often we forget that God is doing it, we forget about God and we begin to worship the reality of what we are seeing. . . . Idolatry does not begin when you take a statue, you give it a certain shape, and then you bow to it and kiss its feet. It begins when you believe that there are those things which exist outside the agency of God; that is the beginning of idolatry and that is the result of nature. Nature means the habit of seeing things happen.[53]

"Nature," for Boteach, is more than just streams, trees, and sky. It is the ordered pattern of the entire world, the face of creation that is repetitive and routine: the sun rising and setting, the Earth revolving and rotating, and yes, sperm fertilizing ova. Because these things persist with some degree of regularity, we tune them out, just as our ears might adjust to the continuous sound of rushing water after a few minutes. Instead, we keep our eyes primed for the unexpected, the miraculous, which almost never happens. Enter disappointment and disillusionment with God. Because we can't seem to trust God to deliver a miracle once in a while, we hedge our bets with nature, which at the very least can be trusted to keep the Earth on its axis rather than spontaneously plummeting into the sun.

I've heard it said that God created the rules of nature so He could interrupt them and clearly display miracles. But this implies nature is somehow in a different category from a miracle. To the contrary, Boteach reminds us that a miracle isn't a *disruption* of natural processes, it's a revelation of what (or rather, who) lies behind them in the first place:

> What is a miracle? A miracle means when God is acting, as involved as He always is, not even more involved, just as involved in making things happen, in being the only existence in the world, only this time He's allowing that fact to show, the fact that He's making it happen. That's what we call a miracle.[54]

A miracle, then, is not a thing in and of itself but a lens, a mode of perceiving God in and through our lives. If the Red Sea were to part every afternoon at the same time, just as Old Faithful erupts predictably every hour or two, Boteach says it would not be regarded as a miracle the way it was for the ancient Hebrews. People would still be amazed, tourists would still flock to take pictures of the Red Sea. But—because it occurred regularly—they would interpret the parting of the Red Sea as a wonder of nature rather than a miracle of God.

Ultimately, our task as creatures is to give thanks, and to do that we must first learn to perceive nature as miracle. Boteach refers to this process as a "breaking of habit," a snapping out of our mindless way of seeing. This process of waking up "brings us to the appreciation that we are indebted to God for everything we have in life." Instead of feeling entitled to the "givenness" of nature, we begin to realize that "[w]hatever we possess . . . should bring us to offer God thanks."[55] Rather than the presumption or just plain mindlessness that nature in its predictability so often prompts, we must learn to *see* all the givenness of our world—all we take for granted or assume is ours—as enacted and sustained by God. And then offer it back to Him in thanks.

What does all this have to do with infertility? This is where the rubber of sacramental theology meets the road of painful reality. As I see it, the phenomenon of procreation is a little like Boteach's Red Sea scenario. We live in a world where, statistically speaking, being able to get pregnant is the norm. It's estimated that some 250 babies are born every *minute* around the world—Boteach thought that if the Red Sea parted once every *day*, we'd forget how miraculous it was. Of course, we still cheer when a couple announces their pregnancy; we still marvel at a newborn. (Incidentally, as I wrote this, the Duke and Duchess of Sussex were evidently giving birth to their first baby. Just moments ago, a wide-eyed, "newly illumined" Prince Harry emerged from the birth chamber to announce his glad tidings to the press and, between smiles and tears, he barely managed to find words for his joy. Say what you will about the state of humanity at the moment, but if the most privileged and media-trained folks in our world are still gleefully and tearfully speechless in the face of new life, perhaps there's hope.)

But for all our baby bliss, deep down do we truly regard pro-creation as a wonder of nature or a miracle of God? I think if we woke up tomorrow to a world where the fertility rates were sud-denly flipped—if 85% of couples were spontaneously infertile and only 15% could conceive easily—we could answer that question with greater conviction and clarity. As it stands, the minority of us strug-gling to get pregnant serve as an important if overlooked reminder that everyone alive on this planet right now is an absolute, sacred, inexpressible, inexhaustible miracle. That there are a whopping 7 bil-lion of us, and 250 more being born every minute, in no way detracts from the magnitude or rarity of that miracle.

Which brings us, or at least me, to a difficult possibility. Upon encountering a blind man, the disciples once asked Christ a ques-tion: "'Rabbi, who sinned, this man or his parents, that he was born blind?' Christ answered, 'Neither this man nor his parents sinned, but that the works of God should be revealed in him'" (John 9:2–3). Like infertility, blindness is "unnatural," less common than being able to see, prompting the disciples to speculate. I venture back to this story when my childlessness tempts me to feel cursed or pun-ished. And because Christ went on to heal the man by restoring his sight, I have also bought into the comfort that maybe that's what all this is for—maybe God is just waiting to reveal Himself by healing my barrenness miraculously.

Maybe, or maybe not. Maybe "revealing His works in me" will mean *not* healing me in the way I request (healing can take a mul-titude of forms) while continuing to grant me childlessness so that it might point to the utter miracle of conception *in general*, not nec-essarily in *my* womb. To borrow the words of Boteach once again, maybe I and this empty uterus are here so that "[w]hen we see that which God repeats often," we will not "forget that God is doing it." We need a dark sky to see the stars, we need depth and shadow to see an image in relief, and maybe we need a little barrenness in the world to see with clarity the gift of life. It is not easy for me to write these words—in fact, it is crushing. I frankly *don't like* that God's ways are often harder—not just higher—than my ways. But the possibility that barrenness can bear witness to God's glory, and that maybe He even ordains some of us for this struggle, remains the single most excruciating and comforting thought I've had in all my years of infertility.

⊗⊘

"If you cannot be thankful for the other gifts God bestowed upon you, you lose your purpose in life. I saw that first hand. As soon as I decided to see my position as one of opportunity, it was easier to handle the aching desire to have my own child. I'm not saying it cured my sadness entirely. But I could acknowledge those feelings and let them go without allowing them to fester into anger or irritation." —Sophia

⊗⊘

"SING, O BARREN ONE"

One of my favorite passages in the Bible has taken on special significance since I began dealing with infertility. Isaiah 53 encompasses a depiction of the Messiah often referred to as the "Suffering Servant" or "Man of Sorrows," and is one of the most moving prophecies of Christ in the Old Testament. In the evangelical church I attended growing up, our pastor read this passage aloud every time we partook of Communion—it was one of very few ritual elements in our charismatic worship service, and the verses have inscribed themselves on my heart in a way few other portions of Scripture have.

Because of how clearly this chapter of Isaiah portrays the suffering Messiah, as a child I assumed it was from the New Testament—looking *back* on Christ's life and death. Not until I was a teenager and began reading the Bible for myself did I realize it was a prophecy, written some eight centuries *before* Christ. To this day, I get goosebumps every time I read these words—their prophetic precision, their sober anticipation, their beauty. Here's a taste of what I mean:

> [H]e had no form or majesty that we should look at him,
> nothing in his appearance that we should desire him.
> He was despised and rejected by others;
> a man of suffering and acquainted with infirmity;
> and as one from whom others hide their faces
> he was despised, and we held him of no account.
>
> Surely he has borne our infirmities
> and carried our diseases;
> yet we accounted him stricken,
> struck down by God, and afflicted.
> But he was wounded for our transgressions,
> crushed for our iniquities;
> upon him was the punishment that made us whole,
> and by his bruises we are healed. (Isaiah 53:2–5, NRSV)

Like I said: goosebumps.

The rest of the chapter continues in much the same way, describing specific characteristics of the Suffering Servant, and concludes with the propitiatory death of the figure we as Christians recognize as Christ, who:

> [P]oured out himself to death,
> and was numbered with the transgressors;
> yet he bore the sin of many,
> and made intercession for the transgressors. (v. 12)

There is much one could say by way of commentary on this moving passage. But at this point, how would you expect Isaiah to continue? Perhaps, like much of the rest of his prophecy, with a call for Israel to repent, to remember God, to turn and be healed? It wouldn't be surprising. But, strangely, what immediately follows this heart-rending vignette is, at first glance, a glaring non sequitur:

> Sing, O barren one who did not bear;
> burst into song and shout,
> you who have not been in labor!
> For the children of the desolate woman will be more
> than the children of her that is married, says the Lord.
> Enlarge the site of your tent,
> and let the curtains of your habitations be stretched out;
> do not hold back; lengthen your cords
> and strengthen your stakes.
> For you will spread out to the right and to the left,
> and your descendants will possess the nations
> and will settle the desolate towns. (Isaiah 54:1–3, NRSV)

How did we get from the Suffering Servant to the barren woman? Traditionally, this "barren one" is seen as the Gentiles, who without Christ are desolate, unable to be reconciled to God, an allegory St. Paul unpacks in Galatians 4:21–31. While the Covenant of Israel was passed down only to flesh descendants of Abraham, the Church would be enlarged through its children born of the Spirit—that is, regenerated through baptism in Christ, whether Jew or Gentile, slave of free. The call for the barren one to sing is really an invitation for the Gentiles to rejoice in anticipation of their portion of the Promise.

But nowadays when I read this passage, I have to remind myself it's not about me. I have to keep remembering that Isaiah was not referring to barren women in general, but symbolically to Hagar— the mother of the Gentiles, the same "barren woman" St. Paul invoked when he said of the Church: "the Jerusalem above is free, which is the mother of us all" (Gal 4:26).

It's hard to be objective about this passage because the longer I myself *live* as a barren woman, I can't help but find personal comfort in the words Isaiah wrote so long ago. I am the "barren one." The commands God gives her become mine: *Sing . . . Burst into song . . . Shout . . . Enlarge . . . Do not hold back . . . Lengthen.* And the promises He bestows upon her, too, become mine: *You will spread out to the right and to the left. . . . You will settle the desolate towns.* The empty places in me will be filled; my small frame is worthy of occupying space. And why? What precisely is my reason to make any of this joy or worthiness my own? It is Christ—His suffering, His Resurrection. Maybe I will never *shout* in labor, maybe I will never *burst into song* at the sight of my own child, maybe my body will never *enlarge* for a baby, but Christ our salvation has granted us—and me, personally—a new reason and ability to do all these things.

As self-oriented as this reading is, it in some way echoes the songs of childless women throughout Scripture in the generations that preceded Christ. When their wombs were opened, many of them responded to God with effusive songs of thanksgiving. The prayer of Hannah, the words of Elizabeth, and, most famously, the Magnificat of Mary amount to some of the longest and most personal passages in Scripture attributed to women in the first person. These songs set up an expectation that when a woman learns she is pregnant, particularly through miraculous means, she gives thanks to God—abundantly. Excessively. But in Christ, as this passage in Isaiah foreshadows, the *barren* woman is called to voice the first fruits of thanksgiving. *He* is the Life we carry within us, *He* is the Good News we've waited for, *His* is the salvation we must continually stretch and grow and make room for in ourselves and in all the world—as though we could ever possibly contain it.

I return to this passage when I am feeling desolate, when the emptiness of my womb makes me me want to pack up the tent of my being rather than enlarge it, when my bitterness shortens the cords of my patience rather than lengthens them. I don't always like what I find in these verses—it is not easy to sing or shout for joy when my throat has been parched by years of forestalled hopes. But that's exactly the point. To be barren is to know suffering, not in our heads nor our hearts but in the deepest, softest part of us. *Sing, O barren one*, not despite your sorrow but because of it.

✺

"At this point, I am quite comfortable saying that I think God has intentionally allowed this struggle in our lives. Even though I see infertility as an illness, I also see that it has borne great fruit in my life, though not without pain." —Teresa

✺

CHOOSE YOUR OWN ENDING:
THE TWO OUTCOMES OF INFERTILITY

While there are many ways one could begin a tale of infertility, there are seemingly only two ways it can end: with a baby or without. Certainly this is where strictly medical concepts of infertility eventually terminate—technically, the condition ends either when the couple is able to conceive, or when the woman's childbearing years come to an end.

Yet when I peer behind the veil, when I consider all that barrenness is and has meant to humanity and to me personally, I see that the biological outcomes of infertility aren't what this is about. I can't help but recall another story of barrenness (of a sort) that also had two potential endings: Israel's wandering in the desert. Their forty years in the empty wilderness finally concluded in the Book of Deuteronomy, the fifth and final installment of the Pentateuch, which traces the creation of humanity and establishment of God's covenant with His people.

Israel's relationship to the Lord God had by this point been born from the waters of the flood, forged in slavery, and tested in the desert. Now the long years of wandering are past, the Israelites have received the Law, and they stand on the shores of the Promised Land. Before they enter, Moses—who will not live to accompany them beyond the Jordan River—turns to them as a father bestowing his final blessing on his children. His words culminate in a crossroads; not unlike a choose-your-own-adventure novel, Moses prompts Israel to decide how *they* want their story to end:

> See, I set before you today life and death, good and evil. If you hear the commandments of the Lord your God I command you today, to love the Lord your God, to walk in His ways, and to keep His ordinances and judgments, then you shall live and multiply; and the Lord your God will bless you in the land you go to inherit. But if your heart turns away and you do not hear, but go astray and worship different gods and serve them, I announce to you today, you shall surely perish; you shall not prolong your days in the land the Lord your God is giving you. . . . I call heaven and earth as witnesses today against you: I set before you life and death, blessing and cursing. Therefore choose life, that both you and your seed may live and love the Lord your God, obey His voice, and cling to Him. For this is your life and the length of your days. (Deut. 30:15–20)

The choice Moses presents his people with is not whether or not to enter the Promised Land—that's already a given—but whether to live or die after inhabiting it. Just when the Israelites think the "real" struggle is behind them, that the Promised Land will magically

UNDER THE LAUREL TREE

put an end to all their nomadic restlessness and fickleness, Moses sobers them up. Virtually the same rules that applied in the desert will apply in the land of plenty; to prosper, they must "love the Lord [their] God from [their] whole heart, from [their] whole soul, and from [their] whole power" (Deut. 6:5).

It all comes down to this: to live is to love God, to walk in His ways, to simply "cling to Him." To die is to turn away from Him, to worship other gods. And idolatry, if we are to heed the words of Shmuel Boteach, is much more than turning to figures carved of wood. It encompasses the entire, silent myth that tells our souls "there are those things which exist outside the agency of God." There is no gray area here—the people of Israel must actively decide how (or rather *whether*) they will live in this new space. How will they inhabit the "new normal" of their journey, joyous as it is?

As we endeavor through these final pages together, it is as though we stand on the shores of our own, respective promised lands—the gates of goodness God has seen fit to lead us each into. Our promised land may or may not consist of a someday baby; it may or may not consist of the things we have asked and waited for. But it will be good, because "we know that all things work together for good to those who love God" (Rom. 8:28).

At the same time, however, we have a choice: life or death. Either we will choose to see God in all we encounter—to see miracle in nature—or we will choose to believe that this situation is outside His care and sovereignty. Either we will choose to turn (and keep turning) to Him with our *whole* being (including our grief, our barrenness, our joy), or we simply won't. Instead, we will parcel ourselves out, giving God only what is safe or logical, distributing the rest to the idols we erect to lighten the burden of mystery.

To me, thanksgiving is the first step toward real life, the kind we are summoned to in Deuteronomy 30. Moses does not mention gratitude by name, but it's there, dancing amid the verbs of the exuberant devotion to God he prescribes: *love* the Lord your God, *walk* in His ways, *keep, cling, inherit.* That kind of life is not one of bare minimums or stingy rations or least common denominators; it is one of abundance—not just God's abundance toward us, but ours toward God. Thanksgiving doesn't wait until the Promised Land to turn to God, it doesn't wait for a baby, it responds to Him even from within the emptiness of the desert.

And that, I suppose, is my favorite moment in this scene of the *Protoevangelium,* perhaps even in the whole story of Joachim and Anna's barrenness. Think about it: Joachim offers his thanks to God *before* exiting the wilderness. He can't actually complete the offering yet—the temple is miles away (see the Epilogue of this book)—but it's an image of what it means to choose life in the fullest sense. When news of Joachim's good fortune reaches his ears, he doesn't immediately flee from the harrowing wasteland of his yearning. Instead, he lingers, sanctifying the desert of struggle by thanking God while still within it.

We didn't get to choose how our infertility journey began—few of us would have taken up this mantle if it had been presented as an option. But, strangely and beautifully, we get to decide how it will end. How can we possibly gather all that's within us—the weak spots, the loose ends, the question marks—and choose life out of all this grief?

Perhaps it all comes down to this: "Rejoice always, pray without ceasing, in everything give thanks; for this is the will of God in Christ Jesus for you" (1 Thess. 5:16). These words, to me, crystallize the whole journey of infertility: don't stop praying—but don't stop rejoicing, either. Prayer in one hand, thanksgiving in the other. If we can manage that, even faintly and brokenly and tearfully, we will—undoubtedly—bring new life into the world. It may not be the kind of life we anticipated, it may not be the kind of life our heart yearns for, but it is life—wholly and holy.

When I choose to travel the path of thanksgiving, I am continuously amazed that God's plans for good far exceed my own. Just think: all that time Joachim and Anna were praying for a child to complete their family, God was envisioning salvation to complete humanity. It's not that their prayers were misguided; it's that the things we long for are often merely a shadow of what we were made for. Our hopes are finite, and God is forever turning them inside out for His glory.

It's a little like the way the figures and objects within Orthodox icons appear skewed and strange until we learn to see the lines of reverse perspective converging on us, the viewers of the icon (rather than on a vanishing point within the icon itself, as is often the case in works of Western art). The stories of our grief often *seem* distorted until we train our gaze to follow where the lines of perspective lead: to us, or rather, to Christ within us. Christ, who has always been and will always be within us. When all seems empty, He is our fullness; when every year passes without a conception, He is the Good News we can share; and when we can scarcely see a path for ourselves outside of our childlessness, He is the way we travel and the One who travels with us.

DISCUSSION AND REFLECTION QUESTIONS

1. What stands out to you about the way thanksgiving is presented in this chapter?

2. In what particular ways has infertility made giving thanks difficult or problematic?

3. What has infertility brought into your life that you can give thanks for?

4. How has thanksgiving helped strengthen unity and reconciliation in your life?

5. What is the most personally meaningful or memorable aspect of Joachim and Anna's story?

EPILOGUE

Recovering Blamelessness

And on the following day he brought his offerings, saying in himself: If the Lord God has been rendered gracious to me, the plate on the priest's forehead will make it manifest to me. And Joachim brought his offerings, and observed attentively the priest's plate when he went up to the altar of the Lord, and he saw no sin in himself. And Joachim said: Now I know that the Lord has been gracious unto me, and has remitted all my sins. And he went down from the temple of the Lord justified, and departed to his own house.
—PROTOEVANGELIUM OF JAMES, 5A

The story of Joachim and Anna's childlessness ends in the same place it began: the temple. The righteous couple has endured their time in both the literal and figurative deserts of barrenness. They have received the promise of a child, they have pledged their thanksgiving to the Lord, and they have reconciled with one another. Now, scarcely a day later, Joachim hurries back to the temple, revisiting the very site of his shame.

Why does he return? To deposit the sacrificial offerings he had previously set aside when the angel visited him in the desert, we assume. But on closer reading, thanksgiving and his sacrifice scarcely surface in this scene. So what is the real reason he goes back? After all, in the eyes of everyone there (read: Rubim), Joachim's situation hasn't changed. These people haven't witnessed his time in the desert, they weren't there to hear the angel's words, and they surely weren't there when he was reacquainted with his beloved. As far as everyone else but themselves (and God) is concerned, Anna and Joachim were still the same barren couple they had been for the last fifty years.

In imagining this scene, I keep remembering one of the literary categories I learned about while studying German in graduate school: the *Bildungsroman*. In English, it's translated as an "educational novel" because the plot usually revolves around the protagonist learning an important life lesson. Stories of this ilk begin with a central problem, often a shortcoming or inadequacy on the part of the protagonist, who then embarks on a quest—either to avoid the problem or find a solution for it. That journey takes him far from home—beyond the Shire, away from Pride Rock, to meet the wizard, to cross the sea, to sail to the new world. After encountering a steady stream of challenges and colorful characters with lessons to impart, the protagonist returns home, older and wiser. It's a full circle moment. Not only do we see with greater clarity how the protagonist has been transformed, but more importantly, they see for themselves. Unlike other kinds of plot structures, the central conflict in a *Bildungsroman* doesn't really resolve or go away; the main character simply gains insight or boldness to face it in a new way.

It's in that spirit I picture Joachim returning to the temple. If this were a Hollywood film, he would take care of business and settle the score—march right up to that Rubim and punch him in the face before daring to offer his sacrifices at the front of the line. But he doesn't do any of that, partly because this was never about Rubim, or the priests, or Israel, or anyone else. It wasn't even about Anna or having a child. This was about Joachim and God. It was *their* relationship that needed mending, their understanding of one another that had to go to hell and back again for Joachim to finally be able to come to terms with the love of God.

"*The hymns of the church, particularly surrounding the Feast of the Annunciation and the Nativity of Christ, are spattered with phrases that sting and stick out more and more as years have passed. The subtext, at least through the lens of this particular pain, is that God is withholding His blessing. There is something wrong with me, not just biologically, but in His judgment. He must not love me. I have not gained favor with God. I am not worthy. The creator refuses to create in me.*" —Emilia

As Joachim looks to the headplate, a liturgical accoutrement worn by the high priest (see Exodus 28:31–33), it's as though all the layers of shame and anguish are peeled away. The taunts, the pain, the isolation, the impotence—it all recedes into the background as Joachim waits for God to reveal Himself. His eyes narrow in on the priest's forehead, and in the twinkling of an eye, he glimpses the object of his longing—confirmation not of a child, but of his salvation. His belonging before God. I see this not so much as a reinstatement of Joachim's blamelessness, but as an affirmation that he had been righteous all along, despite his earlier shame.

In many ways, it's a completely superfluous scene. It doesn't move the plot forward—Anna, so we will learn, has already conceived; the

Theotokos is already on the way. And wasn't that evidence enough of God's favor? But that's the man-befriending love of God, I suppose. Excessive. Unnecessary. Above and beyond. And that's exactly the point. This moment *wasn't* in service of the audience, the plot, the second-century editor who, I imagine, lamented the seeming waste of perfectly good parchment. No, this scene was for Joachim alone. For God, it was not enough just to *be* gracious—even the most capricious masters throw a bone to their slaves on occasion. God had to go and show Joachim that His goodness wasn't coincidental or arbitrary, it was for real. It was love.

As we keep watch with Joachim, it slowly dawns on us that somehow, this was all part of the plan. To be able to stand face to face with God and his wife, Joachim needed to fully bear the cross he had been given: to travel the full journey of grief and behold the grim specter of childlessness and death—not to mention the even grimmer specter of his unworthiness. Just as Jacob wrestled with the angel, Joachim needed to wrestle with God, with himself, with the life he'd been given. Maybe it took all that prayer and fasting in the desert, all that groping toward synergy with God, to finally bear the Theotokos out of the sin-scorched hull of Israel.

What does Joachim's blamelessness consist of? On a cosmic or salvific level, we could say it lies in the imminent approach of the Messiah, whose Mother had been conceived just a day prior. Yet all that, in this particular moment, is a blurry eventuality. For now, it is enough for Joachim to have wrestled, to have fought the good fight, and to have finally come to rest in the peace of God's love. And that is enough for us, too. For us as for him, healing from the shame of infertility comes not when/if we finally get pregnant, but rather when we ultimately surrender to our full worth as men and women, children of the living God whose image we bear and whose love we can never escape.

Dos and Don'ts to Better Support Couples with Infertility

These suggestions are intended to help loved ones and those who minister to offer a stronger and more supportive presence to couples who struggle with infertility. They were compiled based on responses from the *Under the Laurel Tree Questionnaire* and additional correspondences with infertile couples in the Church. While I have sought to list only those suggestions that had broad consensus and practical relevance, it's important to remember that every individual is different and may be receptive to different things.

DO:

» Listen. More than anything, individuals and couples want to be heard and to have their grief validated and integrated into the community that surrounds them.

» Familiarize yourself with the special griefs of infertility, miscarriage, and infant loss if you have no personal experiences with them. Try to understand the unique nuances of this kind of loss rather than assuming it is similar to, or lesser than, other forms of grief.

» Be available and give space. Let people know you will listen when they want to talk, and don't bring up or ask about infertility in every conversation.

» Include childless individuals in baby showers and other child-centered events, but be understanding if they choose not to come.

» Find ways to connect that don't rely on children or the outcome of the couple's infertility journey.

» Inform someone who you know is struggling with infertility of your or other people's pregnancies in as low-key a way as possible. Sending a brief email or text, for example, gives them space to process this news without the pressure of having to instantly smile or exude happiness created by telling them in person or over the phone.

» Keep a person's infertility confidential unless they have asked you to share the information with others. This includes sharing private information as a "prayer request."

» For friends and relatives without children, acknowledge positive milestones and accomplishments in their lives, such as promotions, going back to school, anniversaries, or fun holidays. Recognize that particularly for women in their childbearing years, their own birthdays can be emotionally difficult times.

» Keep praying, hoping, and loving unconditionally.

SPECIAL DOS FOR ORDAINED CLERGY
AND OTHERS IN MINISTRY

» Incorporate the topic of infertility and childlessness into premarital counseling sessions—not merely to identify disagreements around assisted reproduction, but to explore the values and meanings each partner assigns to having children. While one can never fully prepare ahead of time for this scenario, having it on the relational map before marriage establishes a precedent couples can return to later. It also gives an easy opportunity to raise awareness of infertility among couples who may never have to deal with it.

» Encourage both husbands and wives to speak with you together about their infertility at least once. This gives you the chance to support them as a couple—not just as two individuals—and them the chance to share how this might be affecting their marriage.

» Be sensitive about the ways you honor Mother's Day and Father's Day in your parish. Many churches, for example, distribute flowers to mothers at the end of Divine Liturgy, inadvertently alienating women who are single, have no living children, or have otherwise been left out of the "mom club." One respondent suggested reading this address instead:

To those who are celebrating the joy of motherhood; to those who long to be mothers and are bearing the grief of infertility; to those who mourn the loss of children, born and unborn; to those who are remembering their own mothers in simple or complicated ways; and to those missing their mothers today, God be with you. Please take a flower as a reminder that God remembers you all.

» Normalize the condition of infertility by referring to it in prayers, litanies, and homilies just as you might other life struggles such as parenting, unemployment, losing a parent, caregiving, etc.

» Sponsor an occasional guest lecture or retreat on the issue of infertility, not only to benefit those who are actively dealing with these issues, but also to foster understanding within an entire parish. We do this with other difficulties in life—addiction, bereavement, social issues; let's add infertility to this list.

» Be inclusive when discussing issues that pertain to family, particularly in sermons or mixed settings. Not everyone listening will have children or even be married.

» Encourage couples baptizing their babies to seek out godparents who are single or unable to have children of their own. Spiritual mother- and fatherhood is a powerful way to share the gift of parenthood generously.

» Understand that for infertile couples who endure years without any children, their marital struggles may more closely resemble those of retirees or empty nesters than those of their fellow young couples.

» Help couples envision a shared sense of purpose that does not depend on whether they will end up having children or not.

» Encourage both husbands and wives to receive medical attention for infertility.

» Emphasize the "one-flesh," sacramental mystery of marriage in conversations with couples struggling to conceive. This is especially helpful in situations where one partner has a known fertility factor and likely struggles with guilt or the sense that they are robbing their spouse of having a child. Infertility can be seen as a cross they share as a couple, rather than a blight on one partner or the other.

» Be careful when discussing spiritual or religious interventions (e.g. visiting a particular monastery or praying to a particular saint) to bring about children. While miracles and sacramental practices are a part of our tradition, unsolicited advice of this nature risks turning faith into superstition or setting a couple up for doubts and bitterness. My own personal thought: wait until an individual or couple approaches you with a specific prayer, saint, pilgrimage, etc., in mind, and discuss their ideas or questions on a case-by-case basis to determine what would be in their best interest.

DON'T:

» Give advice without being asked to do so (how to get pregnant, what doctor to see, a diet to try, etc.). It is difficult to overemphasize how damaging unsolicited advice can be in the context of infertility—nearly everyone who took the *Under the Laurel Tree Questionnaire* listed this as an unequivocal "don't."

» Make assumptions, even jokingly or hypothetically, about the reason a couple doesn't have children or does not have a certain number of children.

» Present adoption as a cure for infertility. Adoption does not fully solve the grief of this condition, nor is it something every couple will feel comfortable with. Couples should not be made to feel ashamed or selfish if they choose not to pursue adoption.

» Emphasize motherhood over all other options or vocations for women—or fatherhood for men. Don't treat having a baby as something that must be done by all married adults no matter the emotional, financial, or medical costs.

» Trivialize the struggles of adults without children, or assume the challenges of parenthood are necessarily more intense than what someone else may be going through.

» Assume childless people necessarily have more time, money, or energy to give than other adults.

» Point out other couples who have gone on to have children after periods of infertility. It gives a sense of false hope, as does assuring couples that it will all work out in the end.

» Tell couples to take a vacation or stop stressing—it's one of the most stressful things you can say.

» Express jealousy (jokingly or not) about how quiet a couple's house must be without children, how much sleep they must get at night, etc.

» Assume that husbands are less upset than their wives, or that the reason a couple is infertile is necessarily tied to the woman.

» Begin conversations with new people by asking how many children they have. Instead, ask *whether* they have children or (if you are a parent) simply mention your own children. An even more constructive conversation starter could simply be "Tell me about yourself."

» Ask young couples when they will have children, or when they will have more children. This is an intimate and sensitive question and usually doesn't need to be public knowledge.

» Assure the couple that by a certain time in the future (e.g. "next year at this time"), they will probably have a child. When that time comes and goes, they may feel even more dejected.

» Encourage people to accept infertility as God's will. Some people may choose to accept childlessness and move on, others may not, but this is a cross one can only take up voluntarily, not at the command of someone else.

» Refer to infertility as something being "wrong" with someone or their body. Yes, there may be physiological reasons for it, but it's important to refer to people in ways that impart dignity and respect.

» Apologize for having children (if you're a parent), getting pregnant, bringing up parenting in conversation, etc. People with infertility want you to feel comfortable being yourself, just as much as we want to be comfortable being ourselves.

SPECIAL DON'TS FOR ORDAINED CLERGY AND OTHERS IN MINISTRY

» In homilies and other situations, don't present childbearing as a Christian's duty or diminish childless couples for not doing their part to expand the Church.

» Be shocked or affronted by the intense negative emotions people may be struggling with. They feel guilty enough.

» Jump to instruct a couple on what they can and can't do in light of Church doctrines before taking the time to listen to what they are going through.

» Show favoritism or more respect to couples in your parish who have many children. Give voice to the many other ways adults contribute to the parish, society, and relationships.

» Bring up the couple's sexual relationship or offer advice related to it unless they bring a specific concern to you.

APPENDIX II

For Further Reading

Perhaps more than a writer, I am an extremely picky reader. In this appendix, I pass on my curated reading list of works by Orthodox and non-Orthodox contributors (marked with an asterisk) that pertain to key topics that surfaced in this book. I do not endorse all opinions voiced in these works, but on the whole these are the writings that have most supported and fruitfully challenged me in my own journey through this special grief.

* = Works by non-Orthodox authors.

INFERTILITY IN THE CHURCH

Greek Orthodox Archdiocese of America. Challenges in Infertility (webinar). https://www.goarch.org/-/challenges-in-infertility.

Shimchick, Fr. John. "When the Fruit of the Womb is Not Expedient." *Orthodox Church of America* (website). 1994. Accessed June 19, 2019. https://oca.org/parish-ministry/familylife/when-the-fruit-of-the-womb-is-not-expedient.

MARRIAGE ENRICHMENT

*Gottman, John and Nan Silver. *The Seven Principles for Making Marriage Work: A Practical Guide from the Country's Foremost Relationship Expert.* New York: Harmony Books, 1999, 2015.

*Hart, Archibald D. and Sharon Hart Morris. *Safe Haven Marriage: Building a Relationship You Want to Come Home To.* Nashville: Thomas Nelson, 2003.

Mamalakis, Philip. "'Turning Toward' as a Pastoral Theology of Marriage." *Greek Orthodox Theological Review* 56, 1–4 (Spring-Winter 2011): 179–195.

*Pileggi Pawelski, Suzann and James O. Pawelski. *Happy Together: Using the Science of Positive Psychology to Build Love That Lasts.* New York: TeacherPerigee, 2018.

*Thomas, Gary L. *Sacred Marriage: What If God Designed Marriage to Make Us Holy More Than to Make Us Happy?*. Grand Rapids: Zondervan, 2000.

GRIEF (GENERAL RESOURCES)

*Epstein, Sarah. "Four Types of Grief Nobody Told You About: And why it's important that we call them grief." *Psychology Today* (website). April 17, 2019. (Access date: July 4, 2019). https://www.psychologytoday.com/ca/blog/between-the-generations/201904/four-types-grief-nobody-told-you-about.

*Bidwell Smith, Claire. *Anxiety: The Missing Stage of Grief.* New York: De Capo Press, 2018.

MALE INFERTILITY AND INFERTILITY GRIEF

*Anthony, Andrew. "The male infertility crisis: 'My failure at fatherhood ate away at my very being'." *The Guardian* (website). August 12, 2018. (Access date: June 19, 2019). https://www.theguardian.com/society/2018/aug/12/the-male-infertility-crisis-my-failure-at-fatherhood-ate-away-at-my-very-being.

*Barnes, Liberty Walther. *Conceiving Masculinity: Male Infertility, Medi-

cine, and Identity. Philadelphia: Temple University Press, 2014.

*Hanna, Esmée, and Brendan Gough. "'It made me feel less of a man knowing I may never be a dad': the hidden trauma of male infertility." *The Conversation* (website). November 1, 2017. (Access date: June 19, 2019). http://theconversation.com/it-made-me-feel-less-of-a-man-knowing-i-may-never-be-a-dad-the-hidden-trauma-of-male-infertility-84414.

*Hansen, Brooks. *The Brotherhood of Joseph: A Father's Memoir of Infertility and Adoption*. New York: Modern Times, 2008.

*Richards, Sarah Elizabeth. "Men Struggle During Infertility And Pregnancy Loss Too But Doctors Often Leave Them out of the Conversation." *HuffPost US* (website). April 28, 2017. (Access date: June 19, 2019). https://www.huffingtonpost.ca/entry/men-infertility_n_59020973e4b081a5c0fb7b0c.

THE *PROTOEVANGELIUM* OF JAMES

Barriger, Fr. Lawrence. "The Protoevangelium of St. James." *The American Carpatho-Russian Archdiocese* (website). https://www.acrod.org/readingroom/scripture/protoevangelium.

Cunningham, Mary B. "The Use of the *Protoevangelion of James* in Eighth-Century Homilies on the Mother of God." In *The Cult of the Mother of God in Byzantium: Texts and Images*, edited by Leslie Brubaker and Mary B. Cunningham, 163–178. Burlington, VT: Ashgate.

*Vanden Eyckel, Eric M. *"But Their Faces Were All Looking Up": Author and Reader in the Protoevangelium of James*. New York: Bloomsbury, 2016.

*Hock, Ronald F. *The Infancy Gospels of James and Thomas: With Introduction, Notes, and Original Text*. The Scholars Bible 2. Santa Rosa, CA: Polebridge Press, 1996.

MONASTERIES AND OTHER SITES OF PILGRIMAGE

Holy Monastery of Pantokrator-Tao (Ntaou) Penteli (Athens) http://www.pantokratoros-tao.gr/index.php/en/
While there are many monastic centers known for offering prayers for

infertile couples, this is a lesser known convent that I have personally visited and experienced healing from. Originally established in the 9th century as a male monastery, the premises was eventually made into a sisterhood that is nourished by the relics of 179 holy fathers martyred there on Pascha in 1680. The relics and prayers of the sisters have helped bring about healing from a variety of ailments including infertility.

St. Anna Orthodox Church (Roseville, CA) https://www.saintanna.org/infertilty-intercessions
   This parish, established as a shrine under the Greek Orthodox Metropolis of San Francisco, is the only Orthodox parish in North America with relics of Saints Joachim and Anna. Infertility is the most common petition received by the shrine. Couples unable to visit the shrine in person may write them to receive special prayers, vigil oil, and to have their names forwarded to the Theophileon Brotherhood at the Skete of St. Anna on Mount Athos for continued prayer.

SAINTS JOACHIM AND ANNA

Apostolou, Fr. Cherubim. "Reversal of the Barrenness of St. Anna." *Mystagogy Resource Center* (blog). December 8, 2011. (Access date: June 19, 2019). https://www.johnsanidopoulos.com/2010/09/homily-reversal-of-barrenness-of-saint.html.

Nicholas, Metropolitan of Detroit. "Homily at the Feast of St. Anna." *Greek Orthodox Archdiocese of America: Metropolis of Detroit* (website). (Access date: June 19, 2019). https://www.detroit.goarch.org/articles/homily-at-the-feast-of-st-anna.

OTHER SAINTS ASSOCIATED WITH BARRENNESS AND ITS HEALING

St. Elizabeth, Mother of the Forerunner (Venerated: September 5). For her full life story, see: "Righteous Elizabeth the mother of St John the Baptist." *The Orthodox Church of America* website. (Access date: June 19, 2019). https://oca.org/saints/lives/2013/09/05/102503-righteous-elizabeth-the-mother-of-st-john-the-baptist.

St. Hypatius (Venerated: March 31). For his full life story, see: "Venerable

Hypatius the Abbot of Rufinus in Chalcedon." *The Orthodox Church of America* website. (Access date: June 19, 2019). https://oca.org/saints/lives/2011/03/31/100961-venerable-hypatius-the-abbot-of-rufinus-in-chalcedon

St. Irene Chrysovalantou (Venerated: July 28). For a summary of her life story, see: "Irene the Righteous of Chrysovalantou." *Greek Orthodox Archdiocese of America* (website). (Access date: June 19, 2019). https://www.goarch.org/chapel/saints?contentid=498.

In some churches, it is customary on the Feast of St. Irene to distribute apples that have been blessed by her icon for healing, especially barrenness. For more on this tradition, see: Sanidopoulos, John. "Prayer for the Blessing of the Apples of St. Irene Chrysovalantou." *Mystagogy Resource Center.* July 28, 2017. (Access date: June 19, 2019). https://www.johnsanidopoulos.com/2017/07/prayer-for-blessing-of-apples-of-saint.html.

St. Romanus the Wonderworker (Venerated: November 27). For his full life story, see: "St. Romanus the Wonderworker." *The Orthodox Church of America* website (access date: June 19, 2019). http://oca.org/saints/lives/2013/11/27/103407-st-romanus-the-wonderworker

St. Stylianos, Protector of Children (Venerated: November 26). For his full life story, see: "Saint Stylianos, The Protector of Children." *Pemptousia.* (Access date: June 19, 2019). https://pemptousia.com/2017/11/saint-stylianos-protector-of-children-26-november-1/.

Sts. Theodore and John (Venerated: July 12). For their full life story, see: "Martyr Theodore and his son of Kiev." *The Orthodox Church of America* website. (Access date: June 19, 2019). https://oca.org/saints/lives/2014/07/12/102009-martyr-theodore-and-his-son-of-kiev.

ORTHODOX BIOETHICS AND ASSISTED REPRODUCTION

Allen, Kevin. "Struggling with Infertility." *The Illumined Heart.* Ancient Faith Radio. Podcast audio, May 2, 2008. Accessed June 19, 2019. https://www.ancientfaith.com/podcasts/illuminedheart/struggling_with_infertility.

Breck, John. *The Sacred Gift of Life: Orthodox Christianity and Bioethics.* Crestwood, NY: St Vladimir's Seminary Press, 2010.

Endnotes

1   Abraham Terian, trans., *The Armenian Gospel of the Infancy with Three Versions of the Protoevangelium of James* (Oxford: Oxford University Press, 2008), 5–6. Note: in the *Armenian Infancy Gospel*, a ca. sixth-century text based in part on the *Protoevangelium of James*, the lamentation of Anna is expanded beyond most older versions of the text.

2   Andrew of Crete, "On the Nativity I: On the Nativity of the Supremely Holy Theotokos," in *Wider than Heaven: Eighth-century Homilies on the Mother of God*, Popular Patristics Series Volume 35, trans. Mary B. Cunningham (Yonkers, NY: St. Vladimir's Seminary Press, 2008), 71–72.

3   Mary B. Cunningham, "The Use of the *Protoevangelion of James* in Eighth-Century Homilies on the Mother of God," in *The Cult of the Mother of God in Byzantium: Texts and Images*, eds. Leslie Brubaker and Mary B. Cunningham (Burlington, VT: Ashgate, 2011), 163–178, here 166.

4   One study, for example, speaks of three distinct phases of infertility grief. In that model, the first stage of infertility grief is marked by "shock, disbelief, or denial." As the couple moves into the second stage of infertility grief, they "mourn the loss of a child who was never conceived" and may experience "surprise, denial, anger, guilt, isolation, and depression." Finally, the couple "grieves for intangibles: the loss of their self-ideal and denial of expectations, goals, and experiences." Anne M. Hirsch and Stephen M. Hirsch, "The Effect of Infertility on Marriage and Self-concept," in *Journal of Obstetric, Gynecologic, & Neonatal Nursing* (January/ February 1989) 13–20, here 13–14.

5   Daniel Hinshaw, *Suffering and the Nature of Healing* (Yonkers, NY: St. Vladimir's Seminary Press, 2013), 36.

6   Anna Louie Sussman, "The Case for Redefining Infertility," *The New Yorker*, June 18, 2019, https://www.newyorker.com/culture/annals-of-inquiry/ the-case-for-social-infertility.

7   Andrew of Crete, "On the Nativity I: On the Nativity of the Supremely Holy Theotokos," in *Wider than Heaven: Eighth-century Homilies on the Mother of God*, Popular Patristics Series Volume 35, trans. Mary B. Cunningham (Yonkers, NY:

St. Vladimir's Seminary Press, 2008), 79.

8 *Greek-English Lexicon with a Revised Supplement*, s.v. "στεῖρα," by H.G. Liddell and R. Scott (Oxford: Clarendon Press, 1996), 1637.

9 See Hagai Levine, et al., "Temporal trends in sperm count: a systematic review and meta-regression analysis," in *Human Reproduction Update* 23, no. 6 (November 2017): 646–659.

10 Sadiya Ansari, "Male infertility is on the rise—so why aren't we talking about it?" *Today's Parent*, May 25, 2018, https://www.todaysparent.com/getting-pregnant/infertility/male-infertility-is-on-the-rise-so-why-arent-we-talking-about-it/.

11 Sumaira H. Malik and Neil Coulson, "The male experience of infertility: a thematic analysis of an online infertility support group bulletin board," in *Journal of Reproductive and Infant Psychology* 26, no. 1 (February 2008): 18–30, here 24.

12 Numerous professionals and researchers are beginning to draw attention to the overlooked emotional needs of men in infertile couples. For further reading: Esmée Hanna and Brendan Gough, "Experiencing Male Infertility: A Review of the Qualitative Research Literature," *SAGE Open* (2015): 1–9; Vinod H. Nargund, "Time to talk about male infertility and depression," *The Book of Man* (website), access date June 19, 2019, https://thebookofman.com/mind/fatherhood/male-infertility-and-depression/; William D. Petok, "Infertility counseling (or the lack thereof) of the forgotten male partner," in *Fertility and Sterility* 104, no. 2 (2015): 260–266. See also Appendix II of this book for more resources.

13 Rev. Dr. Geoffrey Ready, email message to author, July 4, 2019.

14 Fr. Philip Rogers, email message to the author, June 7, 2019.

15 Rev. Dr. Geoffrey Ready, email message to author, July 4, 2019.

16 Litany during the Anaphora, from *The Divine Liturgy of St. Basil the Great*, edited by Fr. N. Michael Vaporis, published by The Greek Orthodox Archdiocese of America (https://www.goarch.org/-/the-divine-liturgy-of-saint-basil-the-great).

17 My line of questioning here was inspired in part by the paradigm-shifting book: Candida R. Moss and Joel S. Baden, *Reconceiving Infertility: Biblical Perspectives on Procreation and Childlessness* (Princeton, NJ: Princeton University Press, 2015).

18 "The Conception by St. Anna of the Most Holy Theotokos," The Greek Orthodox Archdiocese of America Online Chapel, https://www.goarch.org/chapel/saints?contentid=329.

19 N. T. Wright, *The New Testament and the People of God* (Minneapolis, MN: Fortress Press, 1993), 40.

20 Nikolai Velimirovic, *The Prologue from Ohrid*, trans. Mother Maria (Birmingham: Lazarica Press, 1985), http://prologue.orthodox.cn/September9.htm.

21 Mary B. Cunningham, *Wider Than Heaven: Eighth-century Homilies on the Mother of God* (Yonkers, NY: St. Vladimir's Seminary Press, 2008), 32.

22 Mary B. Cunningham, "The Use of the Protevangelion of James in Eighth-Century Homilies on the Mother of God," in *The Cult of the Mother of God in*

Byzantium: Texts and Images, eds. Leslie Brubaker and Mary B. Cunningham (Burlington, VT: Ashgate, 2011), 163–178, here 165.

23 Ibid., 166–67; c.f. Cunningham, *Wider Than Heaven*, 21.

24 Richard Kearney, *On Stories, Thinking in Action* (London: Routledge, 2002), 129.

25 Rev. Dr. Geoffrey Ready, *Living God's Story: Strengthening Liturgical Participation and Christian Formation through the Renewal of Enacted Narrative in the Orthodox Divine Liturgy* (PhD Diss, University of Toronto, 2019), 43.

26 In his "Sermon on the Holy Joachim and Anna, Glorious Parents of the Theotokos," in *Wider than Heaven: Eighth-century Homilies on the Mother of God*, Popular Patristics Series Volume 35, trans. Mary B. Cunningham (Yonkers, NY: St. Vladimir's Seminary Press, 2008), 139.

27 Ibid.

28 Ibid.

29 Brené Brown, "Shame v. Guilt," *Brene Brown* (blog), January 14, 2013, https://brenebrown.com/blog/2013/01/14/shame-v-guilt/.

30 Tim Horner, "Jewish Aspects of the *Protoevangelium of James*," in *Journal of Early Christian Studies* 12.3 (2004): 313–335, here 318.

31 Mishnah Yevamot 6.8, obtained via The Sefaria Library, https://www.sefaria.org/Mishnah_Yevamot.6?lang=bi.

32 Brené Brown, "Shame resilience theory: A grounded theory study on women and shame," in *Families in Society—The Journal of Contemporary Social Services* 87, no. 1 (2006): 43–52, here 45.

33 Ibid., 49.

34 Ibid.

35 Quoted in: Ellen McCarthy, "For men, infertility often becomes a private heartache," *Washington Post*, June 6, 2013, https://www.washingtonpost.com/lifestyle/magazine/for-men-infertility-often-becomes-a-private-heartache/2013/06/05/049e33ca-ba6b-11e2-b94c-b684dda07add_story.html?noredirect=on&utm_term=.71494603975c.

36 Pierre Grelot, *Man and Wife in Scripture* (Montreal, QC: Palm Publishers, 1964), 11.

37 BD Peterson, et al., "Gender differences in how men and women who are referred for IVF cope with infertility stress," in *Human Reproduction* 21, no. 9: (2006).

38 Nicole M. Roccas, *Time and Despondency: Regaining the Present in Faith and Life* (Chesterton, IN: Ancient Faith Publishing, 2017), 60.

39 Fr. Stephen Freeman, "Orthodoxy and Shame," produced by Ancient Faith Radio, *Ancient Faith Radio Specials*, June 27, 2019, recorded talk, author's transcription, 1:17:22, https://www.ancientfaith.com/specials/ancient_faith_writers_and_podcasters_conference_2019/orthodoxy_and_shame.

40 Quoted in Fr. Richard Andrews, "Good grief," produced by St. George Orthodox Church, recorded sermon and transcript, n.d., http://stgeorgegoc.org/pastors-corner/fr-ricks-sermons/good-grief.

41 Evagrius Ponticus, *Praktikos 24*, in *The Praktikos Chapters on Prayer*, trans. John Eudes Bamberger (Kalamazoo, MI: Cistercian Publications, 1981), 23.

42 Fr. Thomas Hopko, "On Sadness and Grief in Human Life," produced by Ancient Faith Radio, *Speaking the Truth in Love*, November 15, 2009, podcast, transcript, 44:46, https://www.ancientfaith.com/podcasts/hopko/on_sadness_ and_grief_in_human_life.

43 Note on Ephesians 4:26, St. Athanasius Academy of Orthodoxy, *The Orthodox Study Bible* (Nashville, TN: Thomas Nelson), 1606.

44 Others have pointed out the evident intertextuality between Chapters 1–7 of the *Protoevangelium* (which recounts the conception and early life of Mary) and 1 Samuel 1–2 (the conception and birth of Samuel). See Willem S. Vorster, "The Protoevangelium of James and Intertextuality," in *Text and Testimony: Essays in Honor of A. F. J. Klijn*, eds. T. Baarda, et al. (Kampen: Kok, 1988), 262–275.

45 Klein, Lillian, "Hannah: Bible," *Jewish Women's Archive*, 20 March 2009 https:// jwa.org/encyclopedia/article/hannah-bible

46 St. John Chrysostom, *Homilies on Hannah, David, and Saul*, Old Testament Homilies Vol. 1, trans. Robert Charles Hill (Brookline, MA: Holy Cross Orthodox Press, 2003), 75.

47 Ibid., 77.

48 Ibid., 83.

49 *The Office*, "Couples Discount," Season 9, Episode 15. February 7, 2013, on NBC.

50 Christine Gregory, "The Five Stages of Grief: An Examination of the Kubler-Ross Model," *Psycom*, last updated: April 11, 2019, https://www.psycom.net/ depression.central.grief.html.

51 Richard Mullins, "The Love of God," *Never Picture Perfect*, Reed Arvin, Reunion Records (1989).

52 *A Reader's Guide to Orthodox Icons* (website), December 8, 2011, https://icon-reader.wordpress.com/2011/12/08/conception-of-the-theotokos-by-joachim-and-anna/.

53 *Wrestling with the Divine: A Jewish Response to Suffering* (Northvale, NJ: Jason Aronson, Inc., 1995), 142.

54 Ibid.

55 Ibid., 143–144.

About the Author

*D*r. Nicole Roccas has a PhD in History from the University of Cincinnati and, in addition to being a writer and podcaster, she is an adjunct faculty member at the Orthodox School of Theology at Trinity College (Toronto). She is best known for her Ancient Faith Radio podcast *Time Eternal*. Her first book was *Time and Despondency: Regaining the Present in Faith and Life* (Ancient Faith Publishing, 2017). A native of Wisconsin, Nicole lives in Toronto with her husband, Basil, whose efforts to indoctrinate her into the ways of maple syrup and Canadian spelling are slowly paying off. Find more at her website: www.nicoleroccas.com

Ancient Faith Publishing hopes you have enjoyed and bene-fited from this book. The proceeds from the sales of our books only partially cover the costs of operating our nonprofit minis-try—which includes both the work of **Ancient Faith Publishing** and the work of **Ancient Faith Radio**. Your financial sup-port makes it possible to continue this ministry both in print and online. Donations are tax-deductible and can be made at **www.ancientfaith.com.**

To view our other publications,
please visit our website: **store.ancientfaith.com**

 **ANCIENT FAITH RADIO**

Bringing you Orthodox Christian music, readings,
prayers, teaching, and podcasts 24 hours a day since 2004 at
www.ancientfaith.com